THE FORGOTTEN FILM CLUB

THE FORGOTTEN FILM CLUB
BOOK ONE: MORONS FROM OUTER SPACE
by JON SPIRA

ISBN PAPERBACK: 978-0-9957356-2-0
ISBN E-BOOK: 978-0-9957356-3-7

First published 2017 by Jon Spira

Jason! Thanks so much!

THE FORGOTTEN FILM CLUB

BOOK ONE:
MORONS FROM OUTER SPACE

JON SPIRA

CONTENTS

WHAT CLASSIFIES AS A FORGOTTEN FILM?

The FFC is an ongoing series of books exploring films forgotten by society. This is not an exercise in kitsch and not a hilarious plan to 'out' films which have dated badly. It's about finding and exploring films which did not make a mark on the mainstream, evaluating them critically and philosophically, talking to people involved in their production and assessing their place in the world now.

All those forgotten films.

A feature film is not a throwaway endeavour. It's not a doodle or sketch. It's not a haiku. It's not a cake. It's not a piece of creativity that can be dashed out in an afternoon and either enjoyed in the moment or preserved for all time. Any film you might see – any film – was laboured over. A group of people, hundreds of people, will have devoted anything between a few months to several years of their lives to bring it into the world. It will have cost a significant amount of money and production companies, distributors, marketing companies, exhibitors and broadcasters will have done as much as they possibly could to claw that money back and make a profit. It will also have cost friendships, relationships and, in some cases, lives. Maybe it will have created just as many of each. The most insignificant seeming film in the world will have been of great significance to some. Films are flung out into the world to find their place. Some manage that, they land. Not every film is Gone With The Wind, not every film is Star Wars but many have a brief flush of success, or recognition, at least, or fit cosily into the back catalogue of a certain star, director or genre. But some never really land. They barely find an audience, perhaps, or they do so all too briefly and fade into complete obscurity. These are the films which intrigue me. The flawed but not broken. The imperfect but not worthless. I want to know what they meant to the people who made them, I want to know what they mean to people now and I want to work out why they mean so much to me.

QUALIFYING CRITERIA FOR
A FORGOTTEN FILM

1. It must have had a cinema release.
2. It must be, or have been, available on DVD somewhere in the world.
3. It must not have been released as a special edition by a 'cult' label (Arrow, Criterion, Masters of Cinema, etc)
4. It must not have had a published book written solely about it.
5. It must have at least one 'famous' person attached to it.

MEL

Mel Smith died on 19th July 2013. He was one of the most beloved British comedy performers of his generation. He was amazing. He had a great big squishy face that you couldn't help but love as it flicked between expressions of incredulity, confusion, heartbreak and joy. He became famous as one of the four cast members of Not The Nine O'Clock News, a BBC sketch comedy show which was enormously influential and innovative but got overshadowed in history by the event of Alternative Comedy.

When Not The Nine O' Clock News ended, Mel formed a partnership with his fellow cast member Griff Rhys Jones and for the next couple of decades, Smith & Jones were as big as a comedy double act could get in the UK.

His achievements didn't stop there. Mel became a film director. He directed Richard Curtis's first film script The Tall Guy, also Radioland Murders, written and produced by George Lucas and Rowan Atkinson's Mr Bean movie, which was a huge box office success.

Mel was no slouch in business, either. Talkback, the production company he and Jones formed together sold for £62,000,000 in 2000.

Mel kept on directing, kept on acting. In 2006, at the Edinburgh Festival, he played Churchill to Michael Fassbender's Michael Collins in Allegiance, which received great critical acclaim.

But he hadn't been well. A seven year addiction to over-the-counter painkillers, gout and ulcers had left him frail and he died of a heart attack at the age of 60.

The tributes poured in and the obituaries painted a picture of a kind, gentle man with enormous talent and generosity, who had lived a full and impressive life. But there was something missing from these obituaries.

Whether it was to afford him dignity or through genuine unawareness, no mention was given to the film of which Mel's face was the only image on the poster. The only film Mel had a screenwriting credit on.

The initially maligned, and quickly forgotten, Morons From Outer Space.

This book is dedicated to Mel.

FOREWORD BY FRANK TURNER

Like most (Western, middle class) children of the 1980s, one of the more significant events of my childhood was the arrival of my family's first ever VCR. I couldn't now place an exact date on it, but at a guess it would have been in around 1988 or so. I was 6, my sisters were 8 and 2, my father was enthusiastic, in a slightly vague way, and my mother was altogether sceptical of the idea. She thought we spent too much time in front of the TV as it was.

My older sister and I assertively took charge of the new machine. It had arrived with a cellophane-wrapped double pack of blank video cassettes. With the fire of converts, we ripped open the packaging, and immediately recorded the first two films which were on telly. Which happened to be "Grease 2" and "Top Secret!", which took up a tape apiece. I think we actually watched the films as we were recording them. Our newfound zeal then hit something of a snag. For some reason, we didn't, or wouldn't, record over these two films. It might have been because we regarded them as sacrosanct, the original scriptures of our new culture and technology; it might have been because one of us broke off the re-record tabs; it was probably because we didn't know that you could. Certainly, our mother was reluctant to fuel our new habit by buying any more blank cassettes. And so it was that I watched these two films over, and over, and over again. I can still quote a fair bit of the dialogue from both. "Top Secret!" is actually, I think, the Zucker Brothers' masterpiece.

At some point after that (I'm not very good with dates), somehow or other, my sister and I figured out how to get our hands on more blank video tapes, and we started recording (and over-watching) other films. In time we learned how to re-use the tapes, and the collection of films that didn't get copied over was small, idiosyncratic and extremely precious (but always, for some reason, included those first two, uh, efforts). Reasonably early on in this process, I taped a film I hadn't heard of off the TV; I was attracted by the involvement of Smith and Jones, and I liked the title: "Morons From Outer Space".

It wouldn't be entirely fair to say that my sisters and I existed in a cultural vacuum, but our parents' interest in culture generally petered out around the time Churchill died. Modern music and film was just something they weren't very interested in, and so my siblings and I had little in the way of background or context in which to place the new and exciting media being pumped into our home by the radio and the TV. This has led, in time, to some pretty eccentric areas of knowledge (and lack thereof), and some less-than-populist opinions.

I bloody loved "Morons From Outer Space" from the first moment I watched it. In particular, I still think the sneezing in the space helmet gag is one of the best and simplest jokes in all the films I know. It was firmly marked with the hallowed text, "DO NOT RECORD OVER", and I went on to watch it many, many times. I suppose, as I grew up, I noticed that no one else I knew seemed to have seen it, or even heard of it; on occasion, I'd hum the theme tune to myself, to baffled looks from friends and, in time, band members. But then, there were plenty of "classic" films I'd never seen or heard of as a child, so maybe I just hadn't found the particular niche of "Moron" lovers who would accept my critical judgement and taste.

Recently, I finally found that niche, and it consisted entirely of Jon Spira. Jon and I have been friends (and occasional colleagues) for many years, but it's only recently that he mentioned to me his intention of writing an entire *book* about "Morons From Outer Space". And that he was essentially doing so because almost no one else cared about the film. I was (and am) filled with surprise, righteous anger at the injustice of it all, gratitude that Jon is righting a cultural wrong by writing this book, and hilarity at the glorious silliness of it all.

I've read the book you're holding, I've rewatched the film (not that I needed to), and I'm confident anew in my youthful opinion. It's a great film, and this is a great book about it. Morons Forever.

INTRODUCTION

I think that when most people sit down to write a book, they have immediate fantasies that it might just, hey-who-knows-maybe, it-*did*-happen-with-Fifty-Shades, possibly-somehow-become... a *best-seller*.

I am under no such illusion. The audience for this book is so niche, it is currently *writing* this book.

Why does the world need a book on the subject of Morons From Outer Space? It doesn't. Don't worry, I know that. And, yes, I'm fine, thanks for asking.

If you have not seen Morons From Outer Space, it is entirely up to you whether or not you choose to watch the film before or after reading this book. Indeed, you might not feel the need to watch it at all and that's fine. The reading of this book is not entirely dependent on you having already seen the film. It is, to some degree, written assuming that you – that nobody – has seen this film.

When you type 'Morons From Outer space' into Google, you don't find much of substance. On the first page of results, after IMDB and Wikipedia is an essay *I* wrote about the film three years ago. Being apparently the only think piece ever written on the film, it seems that I might be the person most qualified, likely and compelled to write a book on it. So, I am.

Aside from a handful of old reviews, this is the only occurrence of someone writing about the film at *all* until page 11 of the Google search where the film crops up as number 6 in a scant clickbait article titled '9 Forgotten '80s Movies That You've Probably Never Heard Of'. The notion that the rest of the films in this list are to be considered obscure (Batteries Not Included, Explorers and Buckaroo Banzai amongst them) is offensive to those of us who basically watched any films in that decade. Although, to the credit of whichever unpaid aspiring hack spent an afternoon compiling the list on the promise of 'exposure', number 1 is Razorback, Russell Mulcahy's 'pig-beast terrorizes Australian Outback' movie, which is both obscure and fantastic.

In terms of reviews, there aren't many and nothing gives it a rating above 3 out of 5 stars (Empire Magazine gives it a one star, but I give Empire Magazine a one star too, so fuck 'em) In terms of aggregated reviews, IMDB gives the film 4.5 out of 10, Rotten Tomatoes 2.7 out of 5.

We're not dealing with a popular film here.

We're also not dealing with a cult film here because, really, it looks like I'm the only person who has ever gone out to bat for it since the dawn of the internet.

I don't want you to think that this book is going to be the unveiling of an overlooked masterpiece. I also don't want you to think that this is an empty exercise in kitsch. There is a dull trend right now in podcasts and internet articles dredging the sea-bed for shitty 80s films so that a Millennial audience can laugh at the silly haircuts and buzzwords. I have no interest in that. Equally I have no interest in some kind of sub-Justin Lee Collins pop culture quest in which I hound the bemused stars of a long-dead pop culture wreckage to tell them how brilliant they are. This is not a film I want to mock, it's a film I like, it's a film that fascinates me. A diamond in the rough.

So, exactly how much of a cultural impact has Morons From Outer Space made? It's in print on DVD in the UK, Australia, France (Les Debiles De L'Espace), Spain (Los Locos Del Planeta Blob) and the US (where it features in a 4-pack with The Man From Planet X, The Angry Red Planet and Alien From L.A) but it has never been released on Blu-Ray or iTunes. In terms of official merchandise, it appears just three items were made available to the public – a glossy cinema programme in Japan, a lamentable vinyl single in both 7' and 12' (containing the almost-seven-minute long 'Moronic mix' and four minute four 'Dubious version') of the awful, awful theme song. A bastard of an ear worm akin to Agadoo or The Chicken Song. There was also a paperback novelization. But we'll talk about that shortly.

It opened in the UK on 143 screens, including The Warner West End – now the Vue West End – in Leicester Square, which was an 890-seater cinema at the time. It had a proper Leicester Square premiere which, according to Screen International, boasted such red carpet luminaries as king of parody Mel Brooks (who was apparently emboldened by the experience to make Spaceballs within a couple of years, which went on to be widely-regarded as the final word in sci-fi satire. It should also not be mentioned that the word 'Spaceball' is first used in Morons From Outer Space), Superman Christopher Reeve, topless model Samantha Fox, Rolling Stone turned Metal Detector enthusiast Bill Wyman and Rick Parfitt out of Status Quo. The premiere was followed by a party at L.A. Cafe in Knightsbridge. Oh, to be a fly on that wall.

I've worked in and around the British Film Institute for the past four years and never once heard Morons From Outer Space mentioned by anyone but me. It's not part of the discussion when it comes to comedy, sci-fi, British cinema or film in general. It's not part of the discussion around bad films. It's not even part of the discussion that surrounds its stars or director. I have no idea why the film is still in print, especially since MGM, who own it, have consigned far less obscure films, with far bigger stars, to their manufacture-on-demand Limited Edition Collection.

It's a film which had a Leicester Square premiere and a proper cinema release. It's a film directed by a man recognised to be one of the greatest British film directors. It's a film which was written by and stars one of the UK's most popular comedy double acts. It's a film which never, ever gets discussed.

It's a forgotten film.

So, the paperback novelization. When I discovered it existed, I immediately tried to buy a copy. It had been out of print for many years and I was surprised to see that as many as fourteen copies had avoided pulping and found their way to the used section of Amazon. Of these fourteen survivors, nine were priced at a penny. Postage was £2.80, meaning it cost exactly two hundred and eighty times the value of the book to post it second class.

Of the five copies priced above a penny – 49p, £1.50, £1.53, £4.95 and £11.72 (good luck) I noticed that one of them – £1.50 – was listed as 'collectible'. I clicked the link to learn more and it turned out to be signed and dedicated by the author Simon Bell (based on the screenplay by Mel Smith & Griff Rhys Jones). The dedication was stated as:

"To Margaux (my wife) who is not one of the Morons from Outer Space, Simon Bell"

Well… that's weird.

Why would someone feel the need to specify to their wife that they were their wife in a book dedication? Could it have been a joke? Could Margaux, in fact, not have been his wife?

Why was the dedication so oddly unfunny? Why not just 'To Margaux – who is not a moron' – I mean, of course she's not one of the Morons From Outer Space.

Also, the bizarre formality of signing your full name to someone you know? You don't even sign emails – if you sign them at all – with your surname if its to somebody you know. Especially your wife. Or someone you'd jokingly refer to as your wife.

I made it a five minute Google mission to find out who the hell Simon Bell was. I quickly learned, thanks to a Daily Mail Online article that 'writer Simon Bell' had, by 45, never married and had no children. The article itself was heralding the revelation of his new relationship with TV's Anneka Rice. Actually, I suppose it was heralding the revelation of her new relationship with him as he's – you know – not the famous one. They uncover the shadowy figure thusly:

"Bell is a close friend of writer Richard Curtis, whose credits include Blackadder, Four Weddings And A Funeral and Notting Hill.
Described by friends as 'warm and witty' and at ease in show-business circles, Bell has written several screenplays and contributed to the classic comedy shows Not The Nine O' Clock News and Alas Smith And Jones."

I guess he was just Mel and Griff's pal and they threw him a bone.

So just who was Margaux and why did she see fit to allow the intimately dedicated book to slip from her possession? We may never know.

I tell you this story for two reasons; firstly as a demonstration of how my mind works and what you might expect from this book and secondly to complete this contextualization, which might help you to understand the place Morons From Outer Space occupies within our society.

I bought one of the 1p copies.

WHAT IS IT?

So, what is Morons From Outer Space? It's a 1985 comedy about what happens when a trio of aliens crash land their spaceship in England, right on the motorway. It concerns how society treats them. The disappointment of the scientific community that these ambassadors from an alien culture are medically human and also every bit as uninteresting and uninterested as the average man on the street of this planet. The suspicion and aggression from the American government that this is the precursor to an attack. The ineffectual aristocratic bureaucracy of the British government response and, of course the public reaction which is to elevate them to literal rock star status purely because the media has defined them as worthy of attention.

The comedic style is more broad than the premise might suggest and I can't help feeling that this has been the film's downfall. It hides its intelligence very effectively behind brash silliness. I think it shares a certain fate with the film Idiocracy – which has thankfully had somewhat of a reassessment in the light of Trump's presidency. Idiocracy is an incredibly smart and clever piece of social satire which suggests what might become of America if corporations and ambitious idiots were to take power and education and science to be spurned. The problem both films share is that when you purposefully fill your film with really stupid people, it takes on an air of being just a really stupid film because the comedy simply has to be that broad. I can't help thinking that Morons' fatal error is that just too many characters are cartoonish.

Morons From Outer Space was written by Mel Smith and Griff Rhys Jones as a vehicle for themselves to star in.

Smith and Jones, I suppose, were both heavyweights and an anomaly in terms of British comedy. They were both educated at Oxford and Cambridge universities respectively and quickly went into TV comedy, despite both having been more involved in theatre upon graduation. Their professional relationship began when Jones joined the cast on the second series of Not The Nine O' Clock News. Not The Nine O' Clock News occupies a strange place in history. It was a BBC TV sketch comedy which aired between 1979 and 1982, and although it launched both Smith & Jones and the career of Rowan Atkinson, it was not entirely in-step with the era.

The working class voice and anger of Alternative Comedy was fast making the previous Beyond the Fringe and Monty Python generations of Oxbridge comedy seem a bit smug and stodgy. It wasn't until the time Not The Nine O Clock News's final series was being broadcast that 'Alternative' would finally land on TV in the form of The Young Ones and The Comic Strip Presents. The comedy Not The Nine O'Clock News proffered was undeniably funny and popular but it was never quite cool. Whilst not at all racist, it was generally unbothered by political correctness, it was socially more than politically, satirical. Despite being of the same generation as the alternative comedians, its stars were a safer, calmer, more sensible and professional breed. Indeed, by 1982, the success of the show's tie-in record had made them all extremely wealthy and promised decent ongoing careers to all involved.

In 1984, Smith & Jones premiered their own sketch show, which would run, under several different titles, right through to 1998. Their comedy, like Not The Nine O'Clock News before them, was neither in-your-face nor shy and retiring. It was high quality, intelligent modern mainstream TV comedy.

There has always been a tradition of British comedians making a bid for cinema stardom and it has almost never worked. In some ways, Morons From Outer Space sits quite comfortably in an old cardboard box, ignored at a drizzly car boot sale alongside Ant & Dec's Alien Autopsy, Cannon & Ball's The Boys in Blue, Ali G In Da House, Roy Chubby Brown's UFO, Rik & Ade's Guest House Paradiso and Keith Lemon: The Film (which, frankly, is lucky to be in such esteemed company).

To my mind, it actually sits better with The League of Gentlemen's Apocalypse, Steptoe and Son Rise Again and The Likely Lads, in that it's not actually an awful film, it's just that the transition from the British small screen to the international cinema screen was rarely an easy or comfortable one.

As a double act, Mel and Griff never really had a 'thing' – they were famous for their single-shot sketches in which they would sit facing each other, in white shirts in front of a black background and discuss something. Griff would play the gormless idiot and Mel the nominally wiser, but generally buffoonish foil. They were brilliantly talented comedians but as funny as they were, they had nothing that really hinted at big screen potential.

Their roles in Morons seem oddly chosen. Jones is arguably the lead character in the film. Yet the character itself – meek Graham Sweetley – is set up as being an uncharismatic, retiring character in a world full of big personalities. Despite appearing in most scenes, he is often undetectable whilst other performers chew the scenery around him. Smith's fourth alien Bernard is a lovely role, which plays greatly to his squidgy-faced pathos, yet his story runs in parallel to that of the other characters so he is largely performing on his own or with rooms full of extras, meaning there is no real interaction with the rest of the cast. In the film, Smith and Jones only meet in the very final scene. It feels like perhaps this was supposed to be a rather clever choice but instead it's a little baffling and the scene itself is underwritten and a bit of a damp squib after a very funny and abrupt ending to the main story. Perhaps their biggest mistake with this film is the casting of Jimmy Nail, who effortlessly becomes the focus for the audience with his unassumingly raw charisma.

They tried one more cinematic excursion after Morons, Wilt – which was a very different type of film. A dark and more sophisticated comedy about middle class frustration which suited them far better. Jones, in particular, playing a different breed of underdog was fantastically compelling in a performance which eschewed farcical japery for more measured, jaded choices in moments of otherwise broad comedy. Wilt suffered a similar box office fate to Morons and led to Smith moving predominantly behind the camera and becoming a successful director of comedy films – most notably the Mr Bean film, which would propel Rowan Atkinson to international acclaim. Jones continued as an affable, talented presence on British TV, taking on presenting roles in factual series too.

In the context of their career, Morons intrigues me. What was their motivation for it? If they were hoping to become stars, why did they give themselves those roles – both on the sidelines of the main focus, being the trio of aliens who capture the world's attention? Were they more interested in writing than performing? Why is only Smith's face on the poster? What audience was this intended for?

I guess this is my attachment to the film. I do love it but I want to understand its flaws. I want to understand why it is the way it is.

SYNOPSIS

I thought it might be helpful to summarize the plot of the film for those of you who haven't seen it in a while. Or have never seen it. Or never intend to see it. This summary contains spoilers, but then, so does the whole rest of the book. So consider this one last chance to see the film without bias.

A spaceship containing 4 rather humanoid, British-sounding humanoids of questionable intelligence is docked at a spaceport whilst its occupants Des and Sandra (Jimmy Nail and Joanne Pearce, a tetchy married couple), Julian (Paul Bown, camp, nervous and particularly clueless) and Bernard (Mel Smith, sweet but pompous) realize they're a bit lost and in need of repairs.

Meanwhile, on earth, mild-mannered tea boy Graham Sweetly (Griff Rhys Jones) is left to look after the TV newsroom where he works while the rest of the team go out for a liquid lunch.

Whilst Bernard pops out for a quick game of Spaceball, Des gets bored and launches the ship back into space. Bernard is abandoned.

It turns out the spacedock was rather close to Earth and within minutes, Des has crashed the ship on the Motorway in England, somewhere around Luton. Causing chaos on the roads, the ship finally crashes to a halt in a field.

Graham finds himself as the only person available to cover the breaking story so takes a film crew and heads down to the crash site.

Commander Matteson (Dinsdale Landen) of the British military finds himself interrupted at dinner by the news of the crash and is escorted to the site by a police entourage.

Matteson arrives at the crash site to find chaos and all of the emergency services trying to deal with crowds of curious people. As he arrives at the spaceship, an American helicopter arrives containing Colonel Laribee (James B. Sikking) Cultural Attaché from the American Embassy. Matteson and Laribee, who will be co-ordinating the response, are clearly clueless as to what should be done.

Bernard, having sent a distress signal is picked up by a passing alien in a little spaceship. On realizing that Bernard is not a woman, the alien ejector-seats him out. Bernard also lands on Earth, but in rural America.

Somehow swept along by the chaos, Graham finds himself separated from his film crew but within the inner-circle of government investigators. Matteson and Laribee join the assembled boffins at the facility and hear movement in the spaceship. It's Des and Sandra having sex. Outside, Laribee has hired Professor Trusseau, the world's authority on linguistics to work out what might be going on inside. Speaking no English, Trusseau can't understand the request and instead unveils a Close Encounters of the Third Kind style machine for communicating musically. He rips into a performance of Born Free. The aliens hear the music. The door to the spaceship opens. Then falls off. Sandra appears in the doorway to see what's going on and is shocked to find a full military response. The other aliens appear in the doorway. "Did you pull that door off?" Des demands of the assembled experts.

A team of academics and military personnel debrief the three aliens. They find them to be of very low intelligence.

Bernard tries to survive in the forests of rural America. Eventually he finds a rubbish bin and assumes it is the intelligent life of the planet. He gets his foot run over by a car and is picked up by an ambulance and is taken to a hospital. At the hospital, he ignores the staff and tries instead to communicate with the bins. He is transferred to an asylum.

Close observation of the other three aliens has revealed nothing of interest. Laribee declares that they are all being fooled. That these aliens aren't as dumb as they seem and that the aliens have a wider, evil plan. Matteson disagrees.

Behind Matteson's back, Laribee conducts his own sinister investigation – fruitlessly torturing Des to extract a confession.

Laribee takes over the operation with military heft, overriding Matteson's authority. His paranoia drives him to madness and Laribee advocates killing the aliens.

Overhearing this plan, Graham swiftly rescues the aliens. As he loads them into a truck, he is foiled by Laribee who is shot dead by Matteson. Matteson declares his love for Sandra and bursts into song. Graham throws him off the truck and spirits the aliens back to his flat in London.

Matteson fills the street surrounding the flat with undercover military officers. The news reports the siege and the public quickly turn up.

Bernard, in his asylum, sees the news and realizes that his companions are on the same planet.

Graham leaves his flat and addresses the media and public, scolding them for their treatment of the aliens who are our guests on this planet. The aliens appear and everyone cheers and applauds them.

Bernard escapes from the asylum.

Back in London, the aliens have become celebrities and embraced by the cultural global elite. With Graham as their manager, they have quickly become rich, famous and obnoxiously spoiled. Des has become the advertising face of LOOB beer.

Bernard, destitute and wandering the back roads of the US, sneaks into a diner to steal food. On the TV, he sees the other aliens appearing on a big TV chat show. They accidentally let slip that there is a fourth alien called Bernard.

Bernard sets out to prove that he is the fourth alien, but he finds himself surrounded by other people doing the same.

The aliens announce a big one-off concert in New York where they will appear for the public for the first time.

Bernard makes it to the stadium, hoping to get to see his shipmates and be validated. He breaks in.

The aliens have become uncontrollable to Graham – they declare that they want to retire. He berates them until they get dressed for the concert and take to the stage.

Bernard finds his way to their dressing room and hides, awaiting them.

The alien's stage show is unsurprisingly shambolic with a very drunk Des vomiting over Sandra midway through the first song. They leave the stage.

Back in the dressing room, they are reunited with Bernard. Graham observes this. Sandra tells Bernard that they will not share their fortune with him and has him taken away by security.

Meanwhile, in the stadium the unhappy crowd are greeted by the sight of a massive spaceship appearing overhead and hovering down into the stadium. The aliens rush back to the stage to see what's going on. The spaceship's door opens and a man walks down to the stage to greet them. He produces a clipboard and asks if they're the people who hired a spaceship from his company. They sheepishly admit they are. He tells them it's five weeks overdue. When they tell him that the spaceship is destroyed, he says "Well, I suppose you'd better come back with me, then" – they follow him into the ship and it flies away back to their home planet, Blob.

Abandoned once more, Bernard sits dejected in the empty stadium. Graham slaps him on the back, hands him a cigar and begins a business proposition.

CLUNKY BUTTONS

It's funny to think about the things that accompany us through life. I'm 41 years old now and there's not a lot left from when I was 9. My parents, thankfully, are both still alive and arguably healthy but the relationship I have with them bears no resemblance to that which it did in 1985. Thankfully. I set my own bedtime now. Which is why you can usually find me rebelliously snoring and dribbling on the sofa in front of a half-watched episode of Masterchef around 11pm. My sister is married and lives miles away and, also, our relationship has changed. I can no longer rely on the antagonistic bossiness of her 12 year old incarnation. Both the cats from that time are long gone. As are all but a handful of friends who, also, bear little resemblance to the people they were in '85. Looking around my flat, I can see little from my life at that time. In the living room, I have a few framed photos that had existed in my family house from that year and a tatty copy of Where The Sidewalk Ends which I somehow hung on to. Although my therapist would vehemently argue, there's not much of the 9 year old me around even *in* me these days. The sustained exposure to all things Star Wars incurred by making my last documentary Elstree 1976 robbed me of any meaningful attachment to it. The way I view most films and hear most music has changed now. But I still love Morons From Outer Space. And that's not nothing.

It still feels the same, Maybe I laugh at different things. But it still, for some inexplicable reason, makes me feel like 1985. It captured something which other sci-fi of that era didn't. A dowdy British version of sci-fi. Lo-fi-sci-fi. It is entirely bereft of any notion of a digital future. The technology we see here is analogue. Mechanical. Nothing is advanced or in any way futuristic, it's technology which is only slightly different. More Clive Sinclair than Elon Musk. There is something endlessly comforting to me about lo-fi-sci-fi, I don't doubt that this stems from Star Wars. The clunkiness is now the most endearing part of Star Wars to me. Nobody ever seems to notice that stupid box glued to the front of Darth Vader with massive remedial buttons and switches on it. He looks like a fucking Teasmaid. How come you never, not once, see him press them? I love those buttons. Big old clunky buttons with lights in them. And with words printed on them. That's what I like. The Millennium Falcon was full of them. The closest thing we had at home was a big red switch next to the cooker that said 'COOKER' on it. It did not glow. For many years I felt somewhat cheated by the future. All the touch screens and ergonomics and pure bright LED lights. So clean and graceful. No big stupid illuminated square buttons which would make a satisfying ker-klunk sound with spring resistance as you pushed them in.

In 2012, my producer Hank and I were involved in a big motor-way accident in the Lake District. A sudden flurry of sleet threw us, and many cars behind us, into a skid. We got clipped by the car behind and found ourselves spinning uncontrollably across two lanes. The car was totaled. The emergency services were weirdly unsupportive. We stood on the side of a freezing, sleety motorway for over an hour in just t-shirts, waiting to find out what would happen to us. Eventually big lorries came to clear the road and we got a lift to the nearest service station in one of these salvage vehicles. Eight of us survivors clambered into the massive cab and found plenty of seating for all. It was an old beast and full – full – of clunky illuminated buttons with things written on them. I was in shock and would be for the next few days. I had expected to die several times during the carnage that happened on that road – the out of control car spinning in circles, crashing into the central reservation facing oncoming traffic. Smoke billowing from under the bonnet as we struggled to get out. Running across three lanes of still-crashing traffic to get away from the car. Standing in the ice-cold sleet waiting for the emergency services. Getting into that cab, late at night, finally out of the cold, knowing that the worst was over. I pulled the hood of my hoodie right over my head to avoid eye contact with anyone. All I saw was the cats eyes twinkle past on the motorway and the massive clunky, glowing buttons. Green and red and yellow. I hadn't felt that cosy since childhood. For a few days after the crash, I was manic – gleefully happy to be alive, but that ended and I went down low. I got obsessed with the clunky buttons. They made me feel better. I scoured the internet for DVDs of films that might sate me. The Ice Pirates, Starcrash, Galaxina, The Last Starfighter, Battle Beyond The Stars. I spent a couple of days on the sofa watching them, getting my fix. Then I remembered Morons From Outer Space. It had some clunky buttons. It put a smile back on my face.

INTERROGATION

I would never claim Morons to be a perfect film. Not even an imperfect classic. They exist. They usually sag in the middle after the set-up has been beautifully executed or collapse in the final act because the makers felt the need to shoehorn in an exciting story at the last minute. I always call this Three Men and a Baby Syndrome. It's a charming concept and a charming film to watch for an hour; it's your three favourite 80s cinema fellas – well, your one favourite and your two favourite TV fellas, looking after a baby. All the pee and the poo and the nappies and the 'how could a man ever cope with a BABY?' shenanigans. And then, right at the end of the second act, it becomes a film about a cocaine deal and they're suddenly negotiating with criminals and having thriller-style antics in building sites in the dead of night. But if you only see Three Men and a Baby once, you forget all that stuff. The rest of it is great. It is great. I'll fight you if you disagree. And I will win. Because I have righteousness on my side. And I've watched Three Men and a Baby WAY more times than you have, so I really know what I'm talking about. Moving on. Morons is not an imperfect classic. It's just imperfect. But it does have moments of brilliance which punch way, way, way above their weight.

For me, the film has a real highlight, a moment where the purest quality of the writing, directing and performance truly coalesce and produce one of my favourite sequences in cinema history. It still makes me laugh all of these years later.

The alien podule has crash landed and been whisked away by the British military to a secret facility where, together with the Americans, they monitor it from the outside. Eventually the door falls off and the aliens reveal themselves – the first thing being said directly to our species being an accusatory: "D'you pull that door of?" Tests are conducted and the aliens are declared to be human. At this point, in a wonderful montage sequence, the aliens are individually debriefed by a panel of experts before a room full of cohorts. This debrief session, beautifully played by all, proves to be frustratingly unrevealing.

Julian is brought out first in white hospital robe and shoe covers. The first question "Sit down, will you?" confuses him straight out of the gate. Initially wandering over to find a seat in the audience before being corrected. He sits, slightly furrowed brow, very attentive. Nervous smile flicking across his face.

"You have come to our planet from another planet?"
"No, we come from our own planet. Not another one."

This response is met with confusion.

"The planet that you come from?"
"Yes."
"What do you call it?"
"What do *I* call it?"
"Yes, what do you call it? What's it known as? What's it's *name*?"

Julian is slightly rattled by the aggressive tone of the question.

"Forgotten."
"You've forgotten?"
"Yeah. Silly me. I'll forget my own name next... give us a clue!"

The film *is* frustratingly broad in its comedy a lot of the time, but these scenes are pure character. Paul Bown doesn't just play Julian as an idiot, a silly man.

For me the lowest moment in comedy – if you overlook our rich history of racism, misogyny and homophobia – is Mr *Fucking* Bean. The second I see his wide-eyed, high-eyebrowed face, I have to take a deep breath and walk away. He angers me so intensely. Now, I understand that Rowan Atkinson is a genius. I get that. Blackadder is pretty much the apex of British comedy. His Secret Policeman's Ball and Not The Nine O' Clock News work remains legitimately respected. His extended cameo in The Tall Guy. That's... probably... about it. But I'm not just hating on him. Specifically, I'm hating on Bean. He is a nothing. He's not a character. He has no history, no story, no motivation. He's just SILLY. In any situation – ha ha – he'll do the SILLIEST thing. The little shit. What's that? A fly is spoiling your picnic? Fucking swat it, or ignore it. Don't extrapolate 24 minutes of hilarity out of it. What drives me mad is that there is nothing to him. He's JUST SILLY. And everyone thinks it's genius stuff. Like, because he doesn't talk, he's somehow elevated up to the stratosphere of great silent comedians like Chaplin and Keaton. What they had that he never will is empathy. The audience felt them through the screen – felt their longing, their despondency, their sense of frustration. These comedians were also highly satirical. They mocked the mores and pressures of their day.

How did you get me here? Oh yeah. Paul Bown.

Bown is one of those figures in contemporary culture. There are cruel terms for them – also-ran springs to mind – which depend on the notion that success in acting is somehow linked in to fame and fortune. The greatest actors have never, ever – EVER – been the stars. For a star to be a star, it's actually vital that they play essentially the same role – the same *character* – over and over again. If you're not portraying a hero, heartthrob or psychopath, there is no place for you in the spotlight. The great actors, even just the good, solid actors, tend to be on the fringes of that. When I was little, Paul Bown was famous to me. He was on the cinema screen as a moron and he was on the TV screen as one of the co-leads of the sitcom Watching. Watching was about a mismatched couple in Merseyside. The guy, Bown, was a placid bird watching biker who lived with his mum, the girl was – as I remember – just a bit loud and brash. But that was enough to cause comic friction. It was a fairly gentle sitcom but it was well played and Bown was incredibly interesting exactly because he was an anti-lead. I later saw him on a kids TV show about a family of pirates living in a house in the suburbs. It was called Pirates. It was anarchic and surreal and very much in the model of Maid Marian and her Merry Men. I adored it, despite being too old for it. He was essentially the lead in that show, too – playing the patriarchal role. He's worked solidly. He's a journeyman actor. I just think he's really good. And in this one interrogation scene he adds a nuanced, human quality to stupid. The slight moment of internal panic after he says, "I'll forget my own name next". The nostalgic glassy-eyed rueful smile as he remembers Blob. He's better than the role demands. That's something.

Next up for interrogation is Des. Jimmy Nail. Standing nonchalantly next to a blackboard as a boffin finishes scrawling an inordinately long equation. The man stands up, offers Des the chalk and asks:

"Now, can you complete that?"

Des is a little taken aback, gives the board a good long look. Everyone in the room waits with quiet intrigue. He turns back to the mathematician.

"Can you?"

"Of course!"

"Well, what are you asking me for?"

Realizing that his audience are genuinely interested in him and his culture, Des opens up and smugly decides to blow their minds.

"This should interest you lads, this is the sort of thing we have on our planet"

He pulls what appears to be a pen from inside pocket. He approaches the panel and starts drawing on a piece of paper on their desk.

"See this? Now, just by touching this, see? We can make signs, what we call letters and words, yeah? See? P-L-A-N-N-I-T – Planet. I mean, you'd have a bit of a job carrying one of them around in your top pocket, wouldn't ya? And we call this a pen. P-E-N. N."

This scene is the very heart of the film. This film, which is undeniably a mess, has something to say and this is Morons From Outer Space at its most efficiently articulate. Later in this book you will hear people posit the idea that perhaps this film would have been a better 5 minute sketch in an episode of the Smith & Jones TV series. I don't agree with that notion but I'd say you could have lifted this sketch out of the film and, with a little tweaking, turned it into one of the classic comedy sketches of all time. In a few short moments it punctures the readily-accepted belief that any aliens we might meet would be of a higher intelligence, it also shows the utterly vacuous nature of the modern human experience and combines those two things into a gloriously dismissive concept of the entire universe. Maybe it's all crap. All this energy we put into working out the meaning of life and the secrets of the universe – maybe there is no secret. Maybe it's all as dumb and dreary as the day to day existence we all already share.

It's Sandra's turn next, and we join her mid de-brief.

"Ooh Ooh, Show It To Me? Ummmm…. Where Are You Now I'm Up? Temp me Si… You must have heard of Tempt Me Sideways!"

American military attaché Laribee furrows his brow. She stands up and starts to sing a half-remembered rendition of the song "It's such a nuh-nuh-nuh-nuh-nuh-nuh-nuh but it's true. When you are in my arms why does the sky go blue? My heart goes bim-bim-bim-bim-bim when I'm with you. Make my dreams come…." She loses her way for a moment and goes back through the song in her head. "True!"

Meaningless, worthless, drivel scrutinized for any cultural value. If only the makers of the film could have known that thirty years later, pop music would be beyond satire with the advent of "Gangnam style" and "Pen Pineapple Apple Pen" Just to frame that within a modern context; the official music video to Bohemian Rhapsody – long held up as the finest example of a pop song – has, at the time of writing, had nearly 400 million views in the 8 years it has been on YouTube. Gangnam Style, from five years ago, is almost at the 3 *billion* mark.

The scene hits its apex with Paul Bown's finest moment in the film.

"OK, so let's just recap, shall we?" asks one of the academics, poring over the transcript and quoting Julian back to himself. "It's very big, possibly huge, but also wide and round."

Julian awkwardly nods, the academic continues to read his transcript;

"It's a greeny, sort-of bluey, sort of all bright colours, with all wispy white clouds. And, all in all, a funny old place."

Julian smiles and nods.

"Is there nothing else you can tell us about your planet?"

Julian surprises himself and smiles fondly.

"Oh, I just remembered what it's called."
"What?"
"Blob."
"Blob?" they all repeat
"Blob!" he says with reverence.

JIMMY NAIL

When most people think Morons From Outer Space, they think Smith & Jones. But, to me, Mel and Griff disappear a bit in this film – Mel in his own sub-story and Griff into the wallpaper. To me, the star will always be Jimmy Nail as Des. The 'Loob' swilling unreconstructed everyman from Blob.

I have once been in the same room as Jimmy Nail. That room was a theatre. He was onstage, I was not. I felt that I was happier to be there than him. He was doing a short run in the West End production of Jeff Wayne's War of the World. He played Parson Nathaniel, the role originated on the album by Phil Lynott. He looked fucked off. I mean, he always looks fucked off to some degree, but he looked fucked off even for Jimmy Nail. I didn't blame him. He had to share the stage with Michael Praed, Daniel sodding Bedingfield, a 'hologram' of Liam Neeson (which I feel quite confident in saying was not a hologram of any description) and David Essex, who seemed to be competing – and winning – against Nail to see who could look like they wanted to be there the very least. It was a bizarre production in which wee Jeff Wayne, wildly waving his baton, seemed to be the focus of the whole thing with a cast of celebs who wandered on once in a while in crappy fancy dress and sang a song then fucked off again until the curtain call. It couldn't decide if it was a musical or a gig so you had the band onstage the whole time and the actors kind of had to half-act, half-sing for their allotted three minutes of stage time. Oh god, it was... I mean, I loved it because I love bad, bad things but I felt for

Jimmy Nail. I felt bad for everyone in that room, maybe less bad for David Essex because he really seemed contemptuous in his not giving a fuck, but I felt especially bad for Jimmy Nail.

He's better than that.

James Michael Aloysius Bradford, with his massive slab-of-beef face, huge crooked nose, heavy lidded eyes and sticky-out ears, was a star the second he downed a pint and declared 'penguins, pelicans and the Inland Revenue have all got one thing in common – they can all shove their bills up their arse!' in the first scene of the first episode of Auf Wiedersehen Pet.

His character, Oz, was a brutish, belligerent bastard of a man exiled alongside the rest of the gang of British builders to a Dusseldorf building site to earn a bit of tax-free cash. In the hands of another actor, he probably would have been little more than a thug but Nail brought humour and pathos and a hod-ful of charisma to the role.

Nail, it must be said, was not even an actor at this point. An ex-con, reborn as property developer, his wife convinced him to go along to the AWP audition and, through that, he entered the business at the top.

Within a few years, he had achieved that which few bar Nettles, Eve, Thaw and McManus had before him – a regional detective show all of his own. Spender was good, though. Created and written by Nail, it was a dark series with grit and depth and it ran for three series and a Christmas special.

There was a novelization. Nail wrote it himself. *Himself.* Unheard of.

Nail was a star. A British TV star. For a moment, he was the highest paid actor on TV and at that moment he surprised the nation by revealing that what he really wanted to do was sing. So, in 1992 he did with music exactly what he had done with acting – went in straight at the top. His first single 'Love Don't Live Here Anymore' charted at number 3, but he outdid himself when 'Ain't No Doubt' hit number 1 in the UK singles charts in July '92. It was bastard-catchy with it's speak-along refrain "She's lying" to be uttered in equal parts weariness and a kind-of haughty disappointment. In all, he went on to release 15 singles and 7 studio albums. He's well remembered here for his falsetto country song Crocodile Shoes – the theme from the TV mini-series of the same name in which he plays a country music star. I was always a fan of his song Big River which features some lovely guitar wibble-noodling from Mark Knopfler from Dire Straits and Nail singing about the decline of the shipbuilding industry.

Nail is also the beating heart of one of my other sick-day-on-the-sofa perennials, another British cinema comedy which misfired and is hardly remembered, Still Crazy.

In Still Crazy, Nail is Les Wickes, the bass-player of 70s band Strange Fruit who find themselves not-entirely-comfortably reunited in the late 90s. Reluctantly drawn back from his new life as a roofer and family man, Les is the soulful heart of the film. The role Nail plays within the cast is akin to the role of a bass player in a band. He holds the whole thing together. He allows Bill Nighy, and Timothy Spall to bask in the limelight, to get all the best jokes and biggest scenes, yet it's his quieter, lower key, moments which contain all of the real drama because they are so understated in contrast. He also gets to show his musical talents off and perhaps steals the whole film when he sings the song The Flame Still Burns – written by Mick Jones out of Foreigner and Chris Difford from Squeeze.

There's something about Nail. He's a soulful guy. He denies you the opportunity to cast him into naffness as everything he does –

good or bad – he imbues with an honesty that transcends every-thing that surrounds him. Morons From Outer Space is an undeniably silly film and, as the lead Moron, Nail would be within rights to turn in an outlandish performance, but he never does. For all of his drinking, puking and moaning, there is an almost needless depth to the character of Des which his shipmates don't share. Sandra is vacuous – brilliantly so, but this excuses her from needing backstory or motivation. Julian is hazy. He's a bit of an enigma, really. Des, however, is rooted. He is motivated – by boredom, laziness, self-preservation. He's not a cartoon oaf, he's a real oaf. Nail brings a genuine stupidity to the role rather than a pantomime one. He is tetchy, impatient, entitled, but also child-like and sincere.

On paper, Nail's filmography is a car crash. Morons was his first film and he followed it up with supporting roles in The Howling 2: Your Sister is a Werewolf and an adaptation of Robinson Crusoe starring Aidan Quinn. In Dream Demon, an incomprehensible British horror film of the late eighties, he plays a, well, a dream demon. He also plays a policeman in the long-forgotten, but rather charming kids noir Just Ask For Diamond, a gamekeeper in Danny Champion of the World, and perhaps his career high was playing Agustin Magaldi in Alan Parker's adaptation of Evita. Which everyone hates and I didn't see.

People write films off all the time. Whole films. People are quick to say that something is shit or crap or tepid and, yes, that can be the case overall. I just feel that even in really bad films, there are moments of greatness. It might be a shot, or one scene, or a music cue. It might be an edit point or a line of dialogue or it might be a performance. And this is where Jimmy Nail always seems to sit.

The thing is this; He could have done so much more in film. Even a truly awful film can't avoid certain trappings of the medium of cinema. The hugeness of the canvas and the focus of the camera alone will lend a certain poignancy to whatever happens to get caught between them. Nuance is exaggerated. Morons is an undeniably broad comedy, too broad, perhaps. But there's Nail in the middle of it all being real. Showing the innocence of idiocy. The recklessness of boredom. The petulance of entitlement. Think about this: How many times have you seen a 'stupid' character in a film – loads – and it's usually handled one of two ways: it's either broad comedy with no grounding in reality (let's say Jim Carrey in Dumb and Dumber) or it's a sensitive, empathic study of mental illness or learning difficulties (John Mills in Ryan's Daughter). I struggle to name another character in a film who truly reflects the multitude of stupid people I've met in my life. Someone who is neither malicious nor medically malfunctioning but is simply not enlightened enough to be guided by their intelligence rather than solely their emotions. In Morons, Nail's performance is, in turn, brutish and child-like and he transcends the oafish dialogue to show the, well, humanity of the alien.

I think Nail will always be remembered for his first ever role. Auf Wiedersehen Pet's place in the history of British popular culture is assured. It's one of the great working class parables of 1980s TV. I don't know the man, but it strikes me that his approach to his career hasn't changed much since it started – he seems neither ambitious nor in need of the validation of others. He probably just gets on with life and does the odd acting job if he feels like it – in between jam sessions of wibble-noodling music with Mark Knopfler. He's just always seemed so ripe for the picking. His raw presence and his acting choices are so good, no matter the quality of the wider project. I do hope that one day a Michael Winterbottom or a Ben Wheatley will pick him up and give him the chance to truly shine.

BBFC

I'm at the British Board of Film Classification in Soho Square. Unlike many of my fellow cinephiles, I have no issue with the BBFC. I think they do a sterling, even-handed job. They inform parents and consumers about the broad contents and tone of a film and they serve as a useful barrier against what would happen to studio films were they not in place. Film is commerce. Studios couldn't give the slightest shit about the content or even quality of the films they release. Unless the content or quality ties to the commerce – in which case, they're all over it. Half a decade ago, in the wake of the success of the film Hostel and the Saw movies, the studios realised there was a buck or two in the torture porn genre. Swiftly the province of the indie-grime became mainstream teen-film fodder. Everyone has their own moral boundaries and perhaps shouldn't enforce them upon other people, but I didn't like seeing that kind of thing marketed to impressionable young minds as entertainment. My point is: the studios will follow the money. If ex-wrestler The Rock stars in a film that makes a shit-ton of money, you can bet that ex-wrestler The Rock will be cast in every film any studio could possibly cast him in. Even comedies. The Rock. A man with the charisma and acting abilities of his namesake. I mean, at least he's upfront with it. It's right there. "Shall we get an actor? No, we'll use a Rock". I get that this is nothing new, from Johnny Weismuller through to Chuck Bronson, Schwarzenegger, right up to ex-wrestler The Rock, big fucking lumps of gristle have been the biggest stars but... I don't even know what my point is anymore. Oh yeah, without certain things like the BBFC in place, every studio film would literally be The Rock molesting, then dismembering teenage girls in front of a robot whilst drinking a Coke as an Adele song plays in the background. Because that's where the money is.

The BBFC serves a necessary function. Last year, kind-of-documentary maker Charlie Lyne took to Kickstarter to fund a project aimed at shaking the foundations of the BBFC. He was apparently motivated by cuts forced upon the remake of I Spit On Your Grave (43 seconds) and The Human Centipede 2 (almost 3 minutes) and the refusal of classification for the film Hate Crime (the synopsis of that film being, according to Wikipedia, "A group of crystal meth-crazed neo-Nazis invade a Jewish family's home and subject them to beating, rape, torture, and murder.") since these are the only significant acts the BBFC has requested in some time. Enraged by this censorship of – what? Art? – Lyne decided to show the BBFC up by submitting a film of paint drying on a wall for certification. He successfully raised just under £6k (this very book, if you'll pardon my smugness, raised just *over* £6k on Kickstarter), allowing a run time of 10 hours. He duly submitted, and paid, to have the film classified. Which it was, as all films are. It got a U certificate. The idea of forcing BBFC employees to watch a 10 hour shot of a wall is akin to when those tiresome 'anarchists' smash the windows of a McDonalds in terms of 'sticking it to the man'. The man you're sticking it to is usually completely unaware and unfazed and all you've really done is accentuate the misery of the lowest-paid workers who now have to sort out your childish shit for no extra money. Unlike smashing up a McDonalds, however, Charlie and his smug cohorts actually paid the BBFC several thousand pounds to… you know… protest them. So… there's that.

I guess I take the exact opposite view to Charlie: to me, the examples he cites are the reason why I think we need the BBFC.

Why would we want a film like Hate Crime which, reviews tell me, is not art or expression, just a shameless attempt to be as shocking and controversial as possible for profit, to be out there unmetered? Maybe I'm a stick-in-the-mud, but I've worked in video shops in shithole areas and I've seen those kind of films go straight into the hands of children. And adult children.

My only issue with the BBFC – and it is a big one – is that there is no sliding scale on their tariff. The producers of a no-budget indie film getting a one-off public cinema screening have to pay the exact same price as a studio releasing a film with a budget in the tens of millions of dollars onto hundreds of screens countrywide. So, in a sense, they really are denying people the chance to see films, and that is scandalous, just not in the way Lyne limply, but very publicly, protests about.

Censorship? I don't care that they enforced removal of shots of nunchucks in Teenage Mutant Ninja Turtles. I don't care that they refused to allow a head-butt in one of the lamentable Star Wars prequels. I don't think that's fucking with art. I like the BBFC and I like being here.

I'm here to learn about Morons From Outer Space. You see, there's not much info out there about the production of this film. I've found one lousy sheet of production notes – a highly edited interview with Griff Rhys Jones… and that's it. So, I'm wondering if the BBFC's records might yield some interesting results.

As a building, the BBFC is everything you might dream it would be. It's a grand proposition on Soho Square, with a satisfyingly woody reception space as you walk in. Oak panelled, with an old, but well maintained wooden staircase. It's the kind of aesthetic I always imagined my grandfather might work in. A bowler hat and an umbrella stand would not look out of place. As they shouldn't. I'm met in the reception by the affable Jacob who leads me through the building. It's big but narrow. As you clear the grandeur of the facade and reception, you're quickly in a more sixties municipal kind of environment. Everything is neat and clean. I briefly imagine James Firman, erstwhile director of the institution, tearing through this space bellowing "RRRRRRICE FLAILS?" since 'rice flails', or as everyone else knows them 'nunchucks' were legendarily his greatest concern, banning them from sight in British cinemas for the duration of his reign. But I can't picture him because I don't know what he looks like. I do know what his signature looks like, though. Every film of my childhood was prefaced by it at the bottom of the official certificate.

Jacob tells me that the BBFC have been in this building since the Nazis bombed their original headquarters in 1941. It doesn't quite feel like it has been continuously inhabited, though. If you strut around behind the scenes of the BFI, you'll find some things untouched since the sixties. Framed posters and photos from every era, signs and stickers on doors and walls in exotically archaic fonts, piles of crap, stashed in long forgotten cupboards and rooms. I worked for three years in an open office at the BFI with a weird drawing of people in masquerade ball gowns on the wall. One day I asked what it actually was and nobody, of the eight people sharing that space knew what it was, who put it there or why. It's not like that here, though. The building may show its history but the offices are modern, clean and professional. He leads me into the bowels of the place, into a small room with a desk and a chair and a laptop, which is open. On the screen, I can see the words 'MORONS FROM OUTER SPACE' but there are formalities to exchange, paper to be signed, rules to be explained.

Jacob leaves me with my notepad and the laptop. I'm not allowed to use my phone to take photos of the documents I'm about to see, so settle down for a few hours of transcribing. In all, there are 62 documents in the scanned PDF file labelled Morons From Outer Space. The original file, like all the rest, has been moved into off-site storage along with the many of thousands of videotapes which have been submitted for certification over the years. I crack my knuckles and begin to flick through the file.

To begin with, there are some scribbled notes full of numbers.

1577 + 9 + 7 + 4
1838 +3 -30 + 1
1475 + 10 -42 +1
1569 +10 -68 +4
1629 +5 +114 + 1

8090+5

90 mins

(119ft Cliff)

I spend too long looking at these trying to decipher them and Jacob later confirms that those are notes on film footage of the reels that make up the film. Utterly uninteresting but still has the air of the exotic to me. There's a document confirming that the video classification of the film requires no further cuts to those made to the original film itself to retain its PG certificate. Next is a letter dated 14th March 1985, from the editor of the film. The address given is 'MORONS FROM OUTER SPACE CUTTING ROOM, TWICK-ENHAM STUDIOS' – I reckon it's not still called that.

The letter lists some minor changes to the edit since the BBFC did its first review of the film;

REEL 1: A new section of traveling through space. Material has been added to the front of the film. This now carries a prologue.

I've never understood the need for the prologue in this film. It sets a patronizing, unfunny tone (which is quickly sidelined by the opening itself, which is beautifully executed). Prologues and voice overs are often the last thing added to a film in trouble. When an edit isn't working or some bastard wants to leave their creative stamp on a film which they were not a creative part of, these are the additions you'll find. Voice over never works. Not unless you're Martin Scorsese and the film is Goodfellas. Aside from that. It never works. Breaks the golden, immutable rule of filmmaking – show, don't tell.

REEL 4: We have cut down the first interrogation scene with Julian.

Obviously, this upsets me. I would love to see all of the footage for this sequence in particular.

REEL 3: We have shortened the final cut of the reel of Bernard staggering around after his sneeze.

REEL 6: We have shortened Matteson's song as the aliens are escaping and lost a large section inside Graham's flat. Stanley no longer enters the flat.

REEL 8: We have re-cut Matteson's song to Sandra outside hotel. This scene is now shorter.
We have lost Bernard removing food from his mouth after he has been thrown out of diner.
We have re-arranged the opening shots of Bernard on the bridge with the rock, and shortened the scene.

Reel 10: There is a new set of end titles which feature scenes from the film as a background.

It finishes with a note that the new song "Morons From Outer Space" is now being used as a background effect during the scene on the bridge and in the stadium dressing room.

Again, I'm aware that none of this is probably even very interesting to the *makers* of Morons From Outer Space. On the other hand, I'm slightly thrilled to be seeing a genuine artifact from the making of this film. Its sheer mundanity excites me. The changes made to the edit are utterly tepid (except the addition of the prologue, which is dumb, and the paring down of Julian's interrogation, which is regrettable). I move further on through the file and here's where it does start getting interesting: the examiner reports. Four people sat down, in this very building, on the 2nd October 1984 to review this film for classification. Each was required to submit a report recommending what cuts, if any, were required.

The four reports all draw the same three conclusions;

1. An orgasm joke must be removed from the sex scene. There is some hand-wringing about the appropriateness of the sex scene at all in this film but they all agree that the slightly baffling manner in which the scene is shot ("the intercourse looks at first like press-ups") the joke itself is the questionably funny line of dialogue for Sandra "I think I'm having one." If the producers want a PG rating, this line must be removed.
2. The shots of Des "sniffing coke" must be removed.
3. None of them actually enjoyed watching this film.

I noticed that all of the reports included brief critical assessments of the films. I had assumed examiners just watched these things kind of dispassionately, just keeping an eye on potential certification boundaries. "Yeaaahhhhh" replied Jacob when I asked him about it later on, "That doesn't really happen so much now, but back then, older examiners… they did do that sometimes." In this case, all of the examiners felt the need to express their distaste;

"Slightly disappointing, uneven comedy… Griff Rhys Jones and Mel Smith both write and appear and provide what few good moments there are."

"A comedy that offers more than it finally gives."

"Rather one dimensional and only intermittently funny comedy which looks as though it sprang from TV. The cost of the film is hardly justified by the joke."

I'm assuming the filmmakers never got to see the examiners' critical assessment of their work, although they were really no worse than anything said by the professional critics upon the film's release. One interesting point raised by one examiner, which never made it to the point of wider discussion was the question of comedy in the scene where the podule crash lands on the motorway. They make a salient statement that they found it: "Distasteful that within this context we are also asked to laugh at the cars veering off the road and exploding. In no case are we aware that the occupants of the cars are safe." They end up throwing their own thought away by concluding that they had previously passed the film Freebie and The Bean, which does much the same thing.

So, the documents show that the producers were informed of the cuts needed to secure a PG rating. The cuts were made, the film was resubmitted.

I continue through the remaining documents and suddenly my heart races at the sight of a name. A signature at the bottom of a letter to James Ferman himself. The letter is signed 'Mary'. Guys, we have a Mary Whitehouse letter. A bonafide Whitehouse complaint. With all that this lady achieved in not-actually-restoring-the-moral-fibre-of-this-country, I'm stunned to discover that she would set her sights on so low a target as Morons From

Outer Space. But there it is, on a sheet of National Viewers And Listener's Association letter-headed stationery.

26th April 1985

Dear Jim,

I am enclosing a copy of a letter I have received on the matter of the 'P.G.' classification of films. It seems to raise serious questions about the standard set by the B.B.F.C for this classification and I would very much appreciate your comments so that I can pass them on to our correspondent.

Yours sincerely
Mary
Mary Whitehouse
President.

The letter she encloses is a facsimile of one which already exists in the BBFC's files as the correspondent contacted them at the same time as Mrs. Whitehouse.

The complaint, from a woman in Hampshire, is handwritten and dated April 15th 1985;

Dear Sir,

On Saturday, I took my twelve year old son and his friend to see "Morons From Outer Space".

It was a pretty feeble film, but what really concerned me was the scene where one of the spacemen was making love to the space-woman in the spacecraft. This was being monitored by a sound detector outside the spacecraft. It was all rather explicit and both my son and his friend asked me loudly "What is that man doing?"

Living in the country, they are far from ignorant on sexual matters, but this just puzzled them. Afterwards they asked me again what it was about.

While I appreciate that this is a P.G film, apart from going to see each of these films, how on earth are parents supposed to know this sort of thing will be shown??

There were a number of children in the audience and I don't think any of them should have been allowed to see this particular bit of the film.

Yours Sincerely,
Mrs XXXX (NAME REDACTED, NOT KISSES)

The sentence "Living in the country, they are far from ignorant on sexual matters, but this just puzzled them" fills my heart with joy and my head with questions. I should also add that there is something about the construction of the phrase "the spaceman was making love to the spacewoman in the spacecraft" – there is a cold poetry to it.

The Assistant Director of the BBFC replied swiftly;

Dear Mrs XXXX,

I am very sorry that you suffered some embarrassment when seeing the film 'Morons From Outer Space' while accompanied by your twelve year old son. Overall, the board's examiners felt the film was, on balance, a 'PG' rather than '15', but considered that some cuts were required for this category. In particular, reducing the rather comic sex scene that you mention in your letter.

Film classification is not an exact science, but we try to make decisions that in general reflect contemporary public attitudes. The 'Carry On' series of films were rather 'rude' in many sequences, but they were accepted by the cinema-going public as appropriately 'A'/'PG'. The examiners felt that Morons From Outer Space was within this genre, and this decision has been supported by the fact that we have received no other letters of complaint regarding the category of this film.

Thank you for writing,

We do, of course, always bear in mind letters from the public when making future decisions,

Yours sincerely
xxxxx (name redacted, not kisses)

To see the forgotten paperwork of a forgotten film had some poignancy to me. This film has been an enigmatic part of my life for three quarters of my time on this planet. And I've known absolutely nothing about it. Unlike all of my other favourite films which had special edition DVDs issued, books written about them, cast and crew interviewed exhaustively for geek blogs. Any information is new information here. And this has been a good day.

IF FRED WOOD GETS WOOD IN THE WOODS, WOULD ANYBODY NOTICE?

I want to share one more thing with you from my day at the BBFC. I held a little something back. So to speak.

I told you that after the requested cuts of the orgasm joke and the drug-taking were removed, Morons From Outer Space was resubmitted to the BBFC for approval.

Well, I found a subsequent document that intrigued me.

The examiners reviewing the resubmission noticed… well, a little something. The tick-box section at the top of the form where the vertical column lists categories 'THEME, TREATMENT, VISUALS: NUDITY, SEX, VIOLENCE, HORROR, LANGUAGE, DRUGS, CRIMINAL TECHNIQUES, LEGALITY: OBSCENITY, CHILDREN, ANIMALS, BLASPHEMY and FILM AS WHOLE' and the horizontal lists certifications (at this time, in 1984: Uc, U, PG, 15, 18, R18, CUTS, REJECT). The tick against every category resides firmly in the PG column. Except one. Nudity is ticked in the 18 column. What 18-rated nudity is in Morons From Outer Space?

"On video at 00.17 there is a naked streaker with his willly [sic] flapping. A precedent at PG, I should have thought, although personally I wouldn't mind it."

A second examiner says;

"There is however the strange addition of a naked man running out of the crowd to harass the man from the ministry at 17.35 which reveals genital detail which would preclude a PG."

I remember the moment now. Commander Matteson is being escorted to see the podule for the first time, in situ in a field off the motorway. As he walks, the police chief and fire chief brief him.

"Chiefy, how's it going?"
"Hell of a mess, sir. It's attracted every crackpot in the country."

At which point, a naked man appears and hurls himself at the police chief, who gets left behind by the unit marching on. It would be fair to say the 'willly' is flapping and that, briefly, genital detail is visible.

It's actually a really strange scene. It makes sense that a lot of the public would show up to the crash site of an alien spaceship, but this seems to be staged more as some kind of protest march. All of the (clothed) extras are carrying bizarre banners which read slogans such as:

GREENHAM WOMEN SAY 'YES'

IF YOU'RE FROM VENUS, YOU CAN SUCK MY LOLLIPOP

YOU CAN STICK YOUR ROCKET UP MY DRIVE ANYTIME.

And the somewhat worrying

WE COME TO YOUR AIDS

I can find no further documentation as to what happened about this willy issue. The shot is clearly still in the film. Maybe the DVD was taken from an earlier cut. Maybe the filmmakers just ignored the BBFC and were never found out. Either way, it's a strange moment. And watching those few seconds repeating over and over on my computer screen (for research purposes), it throws me back a couple of years to when I was making the afore-mentioned Elstree 1976 – a film about people who had very small roles or were barely visible in the first Star Wars film. I wonder who that naked man is. I wonder what circumstance led him to being involved with this film. I wonder how he felt about being filmed naked and I wonder what he's doing right now, at this very moment. Does this brief moment represent the pinnacle of his cinematic career or is it a long-forgotten moment of insignificant spontaneous bravado? Did he have children and do they know that their father's penis is a very obscure part of cinema history?

I'm racked with the need to find out who this man is and the story behind the moment. My first port of call is Derek Lyons. Derek was one of my interviewees on Elstree 1976. A professional extra in films during the 70s and 80s. He hates to be called an extra. He prefers the term 'supporting artist'. A quick glance at IMDB confirms my memory that Derek was an extra on Morons and, being an active part of the wider community of extras, I assume that if anyone can identify him, it'll be Derek The Extra. I send him a Facebook message. I realize that Derek has unfriended me on Facebook. He does this with everybody from time to time, taking umbrage for bizarre reasons. It pisses me off right now, as I actually need to speak to him. That's why I'm referring to him as an extra.

Then I have a brainwave. While we were out promoting Elstree, I met a guy who told me about a website which is set up specifically to identify journeyman film extras. Except I can't remember the name of it. After some frantic email searches, I find it – aveleyman.com – and what a rabbit hole it is. Each film has a page and every single part in that film – credited or not – has a photo and the photos have names next to them. I search Morons and scroll down and down the page until I find "Naked Protestor" and there he is, face turned away from camera, arm reaching out to grab the

Police Chief. And his name is Fred Wood. I click on his name and a comprehensive supporting artist career spanning from 1942 to 1996 reveals itself. Complete with fuzzy photos of him in the background of so many famous films.

He was in Waterloo Road in 1944, a film that got discussed often at the BFI a year or two ago when the Britain on Film initiative was launched. He was in Gorgo AND Konga – the rather enjoyable early 60s British responses to Godzilla and King Kong. A gypsy in From Russia With Love. He was in Roger Corman's legendary Poe adaptations Masque Of The Red Death and Tomb of Ligeia. I'd interviewed Corman about these films. He was Man Escaping Dalek Mine in Daleks Invasion Earth 2150 A.D. – one of the 60s Doctor Who feature films released in cinemas. He played an undertaker in no less than 4 films, which is beginning to make sense as his distinctive look – gaunt, pale, detached, high cheek-bones, prominent eyebrows, turned up nose all carry a dignified yet creepy austerity. He also does a neat line of people in pubs – most notably in A Hard Day's Night, villagers ('Running Villager' in Robin Hood Prince of Thieves) and general working class figures – from a 'Prol' in 1984 to a dole recipient in Superman 3. And then I notice it. He was in Star Wars. He would have fitted the brief for Elstree 1976. He played a Cantina Patron. And I knew another Cantina Patron!

I send a Facebook message to Laurie Goode, a veteran supporting artist of film & TV history and Elstree 1976 alumnus. He played a Saurin in the Cantina scene but is best known in Star Wars circles as the Stormtrooper who banged his head.

JS: Laurie, did you ever work with a guy called Fred Wood?
LG: Yes, Fred Woods. Loved Special Brew.

We took it to a phone call.

"What d'you wanna know about Fred Woods for?"

I tell him I'm writing a book about Morons From Outer Space.

"Morons from…. I was in that! Yeah, I'm in the woods, there. I'll tell you who else was in there – Bobby Ramsey, he was part of the Kray gang. Mel Smith, wasn't it? Morons From Outer Space, I'm sure we filmed it in Black Park Lake. The woods there."

I ask him if he knew Fred Wood at that point and if he remembered him doing the scene naked.

"I knew Fred, yeah. Yeah, Fred would do anything like that, yeah. He used to take his teeth out as well. He used to take his teeth out, he had no teeth. He had a great character face. He was a very skinny man, wasn't he? He was sort of… Dickensian if anything. Sort of like a poor East End Dickensian worker or a homeless vagrant or something. I can't remember first meeting him, but I think he was doing film extra work from the late forties, or the fifties definitely. He'd been doing it for years! I didn't get to know him immediately but, because of the way he looked and everything – with his big ears – I got to know his face and people talking about him. Easy name to remember, as well, Fred Woods. If he saw me on a film he'd go "Go on, lend me a couple of quid. I'll pay you back when we get paid" and he used to get Special Brew with it. I used to see him two or three times a year, half a dozen times at the most. He's in Star Wars – he'd be an alien, I've got a call sheet, let's have a look… what they say about the extras here… 'crowd: 4 farmers, 3 Correllian pirates, 3 bureaucrats, 4 stormtroopers, local girls, weird girl – that's Pam! – 6 ugly humans.' So, he'd be one of those, wouldn't he? It was a running joke that people would say "Oh, we need a handsome bloke on the film – like Fred Woods. Everyone knew Fred because he was a face that you never forgot – put it that way."

I ask Laurie what he knew about Fred. Was extra work all he did for a living?

"Yeah, that was his main thing. There'd always be a story about Fred cos he liked to drink. He was in (Monty Python's) The Meaning of Life. Tied up on the wall, like a crucifixion, and they brand him – it's in the restaurant scene. They left him there, the arc lights were on full-whack. He just fainted and fell off the plinth that he was on."

"Laurie, as extras, you're not usually asked to get naked, right?"

"Yeah. I've been naked, though. I was naked in a film called The Love Box." He laughs. "It's about, it's a really cheapo film. Oh god, how can I describe it? I was in The Love Park sequence at the end. It's not a very good film, actually. It's about going forward with love… flower power. Who's in it? No one of any significance. Produced by a guy called Tudor Gates and Stanley Long, I think. It's about a guy chasing love and then he ends up happy at the end. And there's a theme park at the end. Of love. And there's a narrator talking over the scene. I'm walking up in the nude with this girl and we're getting a diploma for lovemaking. Do you want me to send it to you?"

I sidestep the offer as politely as I can and steer the topic back on to Fred.

"Easy going, Fred. Easy going he was. I don't think he knew my name, but he always said hello and just wanted to get down to the bar for lunchtime. I just know the odd story but I didn't know him that well."

Back to Google I go. Eventually I find a whole thread dedicated to Fred Wood on a forum on a site called filmdope.com. A lot of people fondly remember him. He died in 2003 and was apparently still working right up to his death. He was a legend in the film extra community – known as The Face. There was even a theory that work dried up for him when he got a set of normal-looking false teeth. His children and grandchildren pipe up in the thread attesting to Laurie's assertion that the man was a drinker. His daughter remembers there were times he couldn't make it back to the film set after a liquid lunch. The thread is full of great screen grabs. On the second page, I find a photo of Fred, in a smart suit, hair slicked back, sat at a table with a familiar man in a white suit standing next to him. It's from an episode of Randall and Hopkirk (Deceased) and that man is one of the show's two leads – Kenneth Cope. A man I've met, because he is my friends Nick and Mark's dad. The thread is a long and jolly read. A eulogy for a man millions of people have seen but never noticed.

Fred Wood stays in my thoughts for some days. This curious, random, naked figure. A man I had never heard about or thought of, despite unwittingly having seen footage of his penis many times. A figure highlighted to me in a pile of documents that have been unread for more than thirty years. A figure I find out, through a day of research, that I'm only one degree of separation from on three counts. It's a small world. Or, as a not-very-wise man might have said; It's a greeny, sort-of bluey, sort of all bright colours, small world with all wispy white clouds. And, all in all, a funny old place.

THE MIDDLE EIGHT

As I've mentioned, there is a song in Morons From Outer Space. I'm not sure the song deserves an entire chapter to itself, so let's call this a mini-chapter. A chapterini. A chapella. What the song lacks in overall quality, it claws back in gusto and bombast. It's a wilfully obnoxious three minutes and twenty-five seconds, played and sung with a kind of flagrant puerility. It's a bad song. But it's also bad on a kind of Timmy Mallet/Black Lace level, it's so bad it stays in your head and jumps out at you at inopportune moments. Years later.

The lyrics are nonsense. The chorus goes;

We're morons, welcome to our pleasure dome
Welcome to our mobile home up in the sky
We're morons, people say we've gone too far

But we don't know where we are, and we don't know why.

I've seen the film, I suspect, more times than any other person on this planet and I have no idea what the hell the 'pleasure dome' they refer to might be. There are no domes in this film. And, the critics have argued, no pleasure. One might suspect a more obvious rhyme for 'mobile home' was not forthcoming. I won't trouble you with further lyrics from the verses from the song, but the reason I wanted to write this chapter... mini chap... demi-chap... is really the middle eight.

For those not familiar with songwriting terms, the 'middle eight' is a section right in the middle of a song – most songs – which is neither verse nor chorus. It can get a bit boring going verse-chorus-verse-chorus-verse-chorus, so most songwriters will drop a bit – eight bars – into the middle of a song. This section will usually be quite different in character and musicality, it shakes it all up a bit before launching back into the familiar chorus and powering on to finish the song.

You know the bit in Sittin' On the Dock Of the Bay where it goes "Looks like nothing's gonna change, everything still remains the same"? Yeah, that. Or the "Oh, let our love survive" gospel-y bit in Elvis's Suspicious Minds – that's a middle eight.

The middle eight in the Morons song is actually kind of interesting lyrically.

Someone out there's watching me and I don't know who
Trying to predict what I will do
What have we got to lose?
I think I'll buy some shoes, maybe a home computer too.

It could just be me, indeed most of this book is, but doesn't that sound like a strangely prescient and poetic summation of the place we find society in right now?

Right?

Right.

Riiiiiight.

MIKE HODGES

"Dude…. Dude! SPIRA!"

I could see her trying to get my attention out of the corner of my eye but I just needed to finish this one edit while I was in the moment otherwise I knew I'd lose track of what I was trying to do, video editing being an intuitive, almost trance-like automatic function of the deep subconscious.

"Jon!"

I hold up an apologetic finger, avoiding full eye contact. There are upsides and downsides to having your desk within 2 feet of your line manager. Communication is exemplary but editing videos to a high standard in a busy open-plan office where people can just bark at you the second they need something is a skill I've not fully mastered at this point.

It's 2014 and I'm working for the British Film Institute as their AV Producer. It's a job title I hate as it sounds like my job is to rig up video screens for events, whereas the more accurate job description – the one I actually use – would be in-house documentary filmmaker. I make short documentaries and interview pieces which go on the BFI's online channels to tie-in to upcoming cinema seasons at BFI Southbank.

On the two occasions I've interviewed Mike Leigh, he has made a point of telling me that 'BFI Southbank' is a stupid name and that he will refer to it only as the National Film Theatre until the day he dies.

I found Mike Leigh to be kind of a dick, though. I know. It disappointed me too.

Dick or not, he has a point. This building, of which my office is in the bowels, is a really strange deal. Firstly, it's invisible. If you're not looking for it, you can't see it. It's on the South Bank, built under and into Waterloo Bridge. From the front, it just looks like a bar, from the back, it looks a massive vent in a bridge, from the right side it looks like a brutalist car park and from the left side it looks like... I really don't know. A big glass restaurant? Naming it BFI Southbank was dumb. Because to the uninitiated, 'BFI' is meaningless. National Film Theatre makes sense. It carries at least an implicit understanding that this is the best place in the country to watch a film. This invisible building has been my favourite since childhood. Every summer, Easter and Christmas, my dad would bring me here when it housed The Museum of The Moving Image, a stunning interactive journey through film history filled with incredible historical treasures and the world's best gift shop. MOMI had closed some years earlier and now the building was a multitude of things. Four cinemas, two restaurants, a public library, a film shop, a mediatheque, a couple of exhibition spaces and a whole load of sub-standard 70s-looking offices housing a multitude of teams from the wider BFI (which had 3 other non-public buildings in and around London). Programming, Events, Festivals, Sponsorship, Facilities, Technical, Marketing all were housed in this one invisible space. As was BFI Live, my team, which consisted of three people at three desks bang in the middle of the Technical department's office. If you've ever stopped to check yourself in the big mirrored window opposite the National Theatre as you're walking to the South Bank from Waterloo Station, well that was our window. And, yes we saw you. We saw you checking yourself out with narcissistic admiration as you barked into your mobile phone. We saw you practicing the first line of your first date. We saw you look at yourself in despair on your way to that job interview. We saw you taking a photo of yourself in the window because you're too fucking stupid to understand how everyone else takes selfies. If you're the annoying bastard who'd turn up with a ghetto blaster and practice your terrible dance moves in front of the window, you know we saw you because we'd call security to move you along twice a week. If you're Sir Ian McKellan, we saw you checking your nose for bogeys that time. What I'm saying is that we saw you.

I spent a very happy few years at that desk making films about films. To my left, at the head of the triple-table arrangement – was my boss Claire and she was the one barking 'dude' at me. I finished my edit, took off my headphones and turned to her.

"You wanna interview Mike Hodges?"
"YES!"

The next season on the horizon was SCI-FI – a big three month long celebration of the genre which was to include a national re-release of Blade Runner, hundreds of film screenings including outdoor ones at Jodrell Bank and the British Museum and lots of bizarre, random fun.

Mike Hodges is a British film legend. He's famous for having directed two films in particular. Two wildly different but enduringly loved films – Get Carter and Flash Gordon.

"We're doing an outdoor screening of Flash Gordon at the British Museum and he's said he's happy to do press or whatever, so if you want him, you got him."

Claire, like everyone else at the BFI, was years beyond being excited by the mention of pretty much anyone that your average film fan would have a conniption over. It takes a lot to get even an eyebrow raised there. I think when it was announced that Pacino was going to do an on-stage, there was the odd raised eyebrow or "Hmn!" but you really did have to get to the point of legendary status to inspire even a flicker. A year and a bit in, I had just about learned to convert my outward elation into the BFI respectful acknowledgement of information and I had definitely learned how to be professional in front of 'talent', but my inner film geek still slipped through from time to time when I heard news like this.

"Oh my GOD, I can interview him about Morons From Outer Space!"
"You can interview him about what now?"
"I love it! It's this reviled comedy he did in like '85 with Mel Smith and Griff Rhys Jones?"

Smith and Jones – the BBC's most popular double-act of the early-mid eighties might have been too obscure a reference to Canadian Claire and her brow was already furrowed at my suggestion that I would interview him about a 'reviled' film he'd made. I changed my tack.

"Did you know he directed a film that Kubrick cited as one of his favourite ever films?"
"Well THAT sounds interesting!"
"Yeah, it was called The Terminal Man, Terence Malick loved it too – it got killed on release by terrible marketing – it's Sci-fi!"
"Looks like you've got your angle!"
"Yeah."

There was a moment of uneasy silence. I think she knew what was coming next.

"But I *really* want to interview him about Morons From Outer Space."

Claire looked at me coolly. She was a great boss. She trusted me, let me make the films I wanted to make, offered advice rather than orders. Even when she'd known I was attempting stuff that wasn't likely to pan out, she knew I would pull something decent from the wreckage and that my lifelong love for both cinema and the BFI itself always guided me to produce something interesting and passionate in the end. She took a breath, raised an eyebrow and tilted her head as she turned back to her own work.

"Do what you gotta do."

Ultimately, I decided to be stealthy. Since I've never once seen a single interview – filmed or written – on the subject of the film Morons From Outer Space, I had assumed that it was in some way a guilty secret of all involved. So I asked Hodges if he'd be up for an interview which encompassed his whole career in Sci-fi. He was happy to do this. I say 'stealthy', I actually, of course, mean 'professional', I mean, I couldn't have just made a mini-doc about Morons for the BFI. Well, I could have. But, really, it wouldn't have been professional.

The day of the interview came. I set up my camera in NFT 2 – the second biggest screen in the building and established a shot which I had done many times before – the classic 'sat in an empty cinema shot'. Filmmakers have been interviewed in this precise manner since time immemorial. I've always wanted to do a supercut of Scorsese interviews to illustrate that his entire life (since he is very gracious with interviews and often campaigns for film preservation) basically consists of being hustled in and out of empty cinemas to say a few enthusiastic words on whatever film, illustrious contemporary or charitable campaign he has been asked to support that day. I went down to the Riverfront restaurant and found Mike, leading him back through the building. A place he has been many times over the years, like any British film luminary, this is kind of a second home.

I stacked the interview, starting by focusing on The Terminal Man, knowing that he rarely gets interviewed about it and is very proud of it. We talked for half an hour on the subject, he seemed impressed that I knew the film well enough to converse knowledgeably, then we moved to Flash Gordon – a film he has been interviewed about a lot. He's very fond of it and has a series of great anecdotes that he enjoys rolling out, so we have fun for another thirty minutes. As our chat nears it's natural conclusion on all things Jones, Blessed and De Laurentis, I smile and warmly say 'OK, if we can move on to Morons From Outer Space…."

"Ah." he says, then starts to chuckle, "Another big hit!"

I smile and wait for him to talk. I'm keen to find out where he goes first, unprompted. The first thing people say unprompted in an interview tends to be the core of their feelings on a subject.

"I think the title doesn't do it justice. When I started making it, it was called 'Illegal Aliens', or something like that. They changed the title. I didn't have any control over it. But I think the film is worthy of a better title"

I ask him how he got involved with it.

"Verity Lambert was head of EMI at the time and she was an old friend of mine. I had written a script, which I've since adapted as a novel, which was called Mid-Atlantic. I'd been running with this script since 1978. Malcolm McDowall was going to play the main character and Jack Nicholson was at one point involved… I'm not a dealmaker. I just can't get deals done, unfortunately. So, I had given it to Verity and she said she'd like to make it – it was a very inexpensive film. Warner Bros were going to make it at one point, too. After The Terminal Man. Before The Terminal Man was released, mind you. Anyway, Verity had it and she asked me if I'd do 'Morons', so I said 'If you do a two-picture deal, I'll do 'Morons', as it was called 'Illegal Aliens' at the time, so that was the deal. Unfortunately, she left before the second film was made. So Mid-Atlantic was never made and I adapted it into a book called 'Watching The Wheels Come Off', which you should read sometime. It's quite funny, I think. So, that's how I came to do this."

But making a feature film, surely isn't something to be taken lightly? He must have had some kind of connection to the material or enthusiasm for it?

"I took it on because I found the proposition that it was making as a very interesting one insofar as if there are other planets out there and other galaxies and the population of those galaxies are ahead of us, in a sense, in terms of their progression... the proposition that Spielberg says, and most other science fiction writers: when they come here, they're highly intelligent and highly sensitive, and so on? Well, you could take the population here and there's a fair percentage of the population who are thick and stupid and insensitive and violent and horrible and so on. The other percentage – well, you're never quite sure which percentage is... there's balance between the ignorant and the more enlightened... you could suggest that they were moronic, these people. So, it was anti-Spielbergian, but the film was also able to satirize fame, satirize education, satirize a whole range of different things – satirize the films that were portraying these advanced species, like E.T and so on. And the Spielbergian vision of the world, which is sentimental in my opinion. I'm afraid this horrible old cynic which is in me enjoyed satirizing all of these things."

I tell him that one of the things that I think the film does, which I've only ever seen done once since, in Edgar Wright's film Hot Fuzz, is satirizing not just the films but satirizing the notion that a British cinema audience can engage with Hollywood. I tell him I love that he brought a Hollywood science fiction film to the British motorway. To small-town England. Was that the point? Was it satirizing the relationship between Hollywood and Britain?

"I can see where you're coming from," he starts. "I can't say... I mean, inevitably because I'm a moderately experienced film director, I would bring the values that I think are important to the film, which inevitably have a touch of Hollywood, although I think I'm a much more European director – for my serious work, certainly. So, you may be right. I wasn't conscious of it at the time, I must be honest."

So, how was working with Mel and Griff?

"Working with Mel and Griff, it was fine... I enjoyed working with them as actors, they were both terrific, uh, it got a bit strained once they'd seen the partial cut." He sighs. "I wish Griff and Mel had taken it just a fraction more seriously. Because when the MI5 and the CIA got involved, I tried my best to make it work and they were so busy they couldn't come back to the script. In the middle of it all they looked at the rough cut and thought that I was shooting it too wide and that it was too restrained. I think comedy comes from... it has to be rooted in a sort-of reality so I don't like over-acting. And because they were concerned that, because I wasn't necessarily a great comedic director, that it was too subtle. And I allowed a couple of performances, I think, to get slightly out of hand. For my taste. First of all, you should never show a cut before the film is finished EVER, they always say "Don't worry, we know what it's like..." but they didn't really know about *cinema* really. Which is why *I* was there. It was as if they'd never seen a Tati film. I was a great fan of Jacques Tati and he played a lot of stuff wide. So, you could see what was going on."

Another sigh.

"But we managed, you know? There were no hard words or anything like that. But, unlike with Flash Gordon where I was improvising and adding things and I would... when they put the sword into the prince I said 'Let's not have red blood, let's have blue blood, he's an aristocrat' – all sorts of little details, but with this one, whenever I did... there's a line at the very beginning of the film when the spaceship lands on the motorway and this car overturns and it was such a violent scene, I thought I'd better add something, so I had the woman say she thought the driver must have been Belgian. Because the Belgians were renowned as terrible drivers because they didn't have to pass a test. And Mel didn't like me adding things without, you know... other than that, it was fine. I was still director and adding things but not quite in the same way. The script was fairly sacrosanct for them, I think."

So, how was the film received critically?

"I had the best review I've ever had in my life. He said "Die before you see this film", which is one of the best reviews I've ever had. The British critics didn't like it, I don't know what it was. Maybe it was the title. Or maybe it's just too broad. But, in fact, in terms of the details of the film, it's full of all sorts of interesting ideas, actually! Albeit comedic ideas. So, I don't know. It's interesting that in America they really liked this film, actually. It wasn't successful. But American critics took it much more seriously."

"It's a film that doesn't get talked about a lot," I say, "What happened to it?"

Mike chuckles to himself.

"No, it certainly doesn't." Again, he sighs. "I don't know. It's mysterious, in a sense, isn't it, as to what survives and what doesn't survive? The critic who said, "Die before you see this film", every time I see him, I say "You'll change your mind one day!" "NO, I WON'T!" I don't know. I think the title is unfortunate, really. Probably. In this country, anyway. The satire is pretty scabrous. It's quite strong about other films. There was a song at the end too, "Morons-da-da-da" that I could have done without to be truthful, but by this time I had sold my soul to commerce and I felt I'd better go along the whole hog, actually. But, anyway... there we are."

It's quite a pointed "there we are" which tonally is a polite "let's move on". But I have one more question for him.

How does he feel about Morons From Outer Space now?

"I think two thirds of that film is really interesting, actually. There's the... song... that I would love to have got rid of, but I couldn't get out of it. I shortened it and shortened it but couldn't get out of it. But the ending is also wonderful, I think." He pauses and smiles. "I like this film. I think because it's so broad and because of the title, people didn't... *pay attention*. If you pay attention to the film, it's filled with really interesting stuff.

I nod in agreement and turn the camera off. We have a chat as I walk him back to the Riverfront cafe. He tells me that, for the first time since he was done with it, he kind of wants to rewatch Morons now. I tell him he should. I also tell him that I have friends who run some of London's film clubs and that if he was up for it, I'm fairly sure I could put on a 35mm screening in central London if he might be up for a Q&A afterwards. He says maybe. He wants to watch it first. We correspond briefly by email for the next week or two. Eventually I mention that I was serious about putting on a screening. He very politely declines.

CRITICAL APPRAISAL

As I'm writing this book, I realise that I am compromised. Critically compromised. I often profess my love for this film, but loving something does not mean it's good. There are people in this world who love imprisoned serial killers, heroin and the music of Coldplay. But this is a different matter. Do the things you loved before you developed critical facilities make sense in your adult world? In the publicity tours that surrounded the release of Elstree 1976, I glad-handed many very nice people who were not children yet were wearing a lot of heavily-branded Star Wars clothing. In conversation, they'd often reveal that they were members of the UK Garrison – a massive club of people who wear Stormtrooper outfits and do an admirable job raising significant amounts of money for charity. I kept wondering why they loved Star Wars. I love Star Wars. In a far lesser way. But I've never defined myself by that. I wonder this about a lot of adult obsessions – football, trainspotting, model airplane making. Trifle. Spaghetti hoops. I wonder if we love these things into adulthood because we've just never stopped to question them. I wonder if we took a moment to really intellectualize them as our adult selves, would they just fall apart? Spaghetti hoops definitely do.

So, I must stop to question Morons From Outer Space. It seems the best way of gaining perspective is to invite the perspective of others. Of experts. I'm fortunate to have a circle of friends in London involved in all different areas of the film industry. I sought their counsel.

You can't get more highbrow, in terms of film criticism, than Sight & Sound Magazine. Since 1934, the British Film Institute has published it to keep the more discerning cineaste informed of film with a wider remit than mere Hollywood. In 1991, they merged their Monthly Film Bulletin magazine into S&S, giving it its now-familiar format of reviewing every single film that is released into UK cinemas, including an extended cast & crew list and a full plot breakdown so rife with spoilers that it practically sits there like a big flashing red button with "DO NOT PUSH" written on it, defying you not to destroy your evening's viewing. Their reviews are comprehensive, thoughtful and steeped in a deep knowledge and understanding of cinema.

Anton Bitel is one of the stable of S&S reviewers. He also writes for Little White Lies – S&S's hipper, younger cousin, Film4, New Empress and many other estimable publications. I send him a copy of Morons on DVD and he agrees to cast a professional eye over it. Having fallen asleep midway through his first attempt, he watches the whole film again a week later.

He seems deeply amused that I'm writing this book. After his second viewing, he's been online hunting for information on the film and, predictably, only found the piece I wrote for the BFI.

"I think you're the film's sole champion in the world", he chuckles down the phone, "and I love the idea that presumably, as a result of this book, you are going to encourage people to look at this film again and they're all going to hate you."

I see.

We get straight into discussing the film and he seems almost pained as he talks about it.

"I think I liked for about the first 10 minutes. Probably up until the point where they crash land and have their very first contact with humans. I think I was *sort of* enjoying it until that point, and then realized it could stop. Because it is just the same joke – the joke encapsulated in the title – told over and over and over again in different forms, and the forms, I didn't really think, evolved very much"

Anton is a smart – and fair – guy. I get the creeping sensation that I might just be an idiot.

"I know it goes through variations", he continues, "I didn't feel it was sophisticated enough. There's a limit to how sophisticated the film can be given that it's predicated on a sort of universal idiocy, but that's a structural flaw in the film for me. They should have found a way to be more sophisticated."

The subject of the film's title is one that Anton returns to several times in the conversation.

"The title is the entire film", he tells me, "There's no surprise left once you've seen that title. In a way, it's a very honest title – it tells you exactly what you're going to get. That is the film and that's what the film delivers. But it would be much more interesting, even though it doesn't take you very long, to discover that for yourself and not to feel that it's all set out for you."

I ask him if there was anything he actually liked about the film. He thinks for a moment.

"The only surprise in the film is the notion that outer space is redefined from the aliens perspective and that we as much belong to outer space as the visiting aliens. That we're the aliens and we're the morons as much as they are. There's a kind of sweet reflection going on between the other and the self. In the scene where they're being interrogated – Julian, the one of indeterminate gender – is asked "You've come to our planet from another planet?" and he says "No, we've come to your planet from our own planet, not another one" – and that's the moment where you start seeing notions of what outer space is, and what an alien is, being switched. And there was one other thing, a gag, a sight gag. You notice the number on the side of the spaceship that they're in is LR4D – which is 'Laugh or die' if you say it quickly. I don't know if that's an actual thing, but I just saw that and thought that has to be a gag."

"So, there was very little you liked about the film, then?"

It turns out there was something.

"I'm a great collector of dismal sex scenes and it has one of the most dismal sex scenes I think I've ever seen – the one between Desmond and Sandra, you find out they are husband and wife and they just go through the most depressing, mechanical sex together, with neither of them remotely engaged and you get the impression that they've been doing this for a long time, just to pass time until someone opens the ship. Because that's what they do. I kind of like that."

Dismal sex aside, Anton has little time for the rest of Morons From Outer Space. He doesn't care for the direction, doesn't think it transcends its TV origins and thinks it throws away the more interesting things it has to say about Anglo-American relations.

"The whole film is just a series of throwaway gags, I don't think there's much substance to it beyond that very neat-at-first and then very banal observation that we're all a bit moronic. And, well, I just don't like films that really convey their point very early on and keep repeating it, and I might add that it's not just because it's lowbrow, I mean this is a problem that I have with much higher-brow films. I had exactly the same problem with Hard To Be a God, which is nothing like this film but I just felt that after 20 minutes I got everything the film had to say and then there was another two and a half hours of exactly the same thing."

"So, Morons is a bad film?" I ask.

"I don't really like calling films good or bad." he sighs. "I legitimately dislike this film. I re-watched it hoping that I'd find that thing that I'd missed the first time and I didn't. I no longer write snark. There are so many people who have worked so hard, it's not fair. You have to take films for what they are and you have to honour that to some degree, whether you like the film or not. I wouldn't want to exclude somebody else from seeing it who had different tastes to my own. I think I would say that if the title is a hook for you, then you're probably going to like the film. Because I do think the title actually is an unusually straightforward advertisement of what the film is like. Not just in terms of content but also in terms of tone and expectation. If you want to see a film that's about morons and you think that would be really funny, then this is the film for you. It's definitely going to give you that."

We continue chatting and he clearly detects some disappointment in my voice that Morons has failed to delight him on any level other than that of its dismal sex scene and he rounds off our conversation with a salient sentiment;

"The reason that I don't like saying whether a film is good or bad in part is because it doesn't matter. It doesn't matter what anyone thinks about anything."

He is, of course, right and refreshingly honest considering how he makes his living, but I can't be placated. It matters to me. I need the validation of my peers on this one. I can't accept that I've spent this many years loving a genuinely awful film. Perhaps it was setting. Perhaps a professional film critic sat alone in front of his TV was the wrong viewing environment. Perhaps this film demands beers and snacks and good humour.

I invite two more from my social film circle over to the flat for a screening of Morons. Hank Starrs is one of my best friends, he is the producer of my films and by far the person I most discuss cultural matters with. Our tastes in film, literature, art and music are different but we both regularly introduce each other to new examples of each and spend a lot of time picking those apart. Although we don't always agree, I have always respected his opinion, which I can never remember being pat or simple. Hank will gladly acknowledge the complexity of anything placed in front of him and is rarely dismissive.

Stuart Barr is a film critic. Mark Kermode has a special fondness for him, regularly mentioning him in his books and think pieces. Stu is a forthright and insightful critic. He adores horror and is as happy to engage with the low-brow as the high-brow. Stu is loud and abrasive and loves a ruckus, always willing to accept a reasonable counter-argument with comic begrudgement.

Both are older than me – Hank by a decade, Stu by seven years. They both remember Morons being released in cinemas and both were old enough to think it looked worthy of avoidance. Neither have ever seen the film subsequently.

Hank was thrilled to be invited to watch the film, he knows about the book and is intrigued as to what is motivating me to write it. I decide not to tell Stu which film will be watched, instead mentioning 'an undisclosed film to watch and discuss'. Stu's response to my email was "It's Morons From Outer Space, isn't it?" – he remembers being incredulous that the BFI three years ago had commissioned me to write an essay on the film for their website.

He was right, but I did not confirm this until his arrival. He was not in any way surprised.

The hummus is opened, the chips decanted into bowls, the beers pulled from the fridge and the lights dimmed. I hear them each take a deep breath.

For the next 90 minutes, they certainly both engage with the film, there is loud, raucous laughing, repeated cries of "WHAT?!?!?!?" and hushed intonations of "Jesus"

The lights back on, bladders drained, weary looks exchanged, we sit down to dissect it.

"So…" I start, waiting for somebody to begin the dissection. They both have wide-eyed fixed grins on their faces, paralyzed by uncertainty. Stu is the first to break.

S: How did somebody say "Yeah, we have a script, let's finance this!"?

H: That's what I was thinking – who read this script and said "Yeah, sure." It was a jarring oddity. It looked like a film but they were kind of running around like they were on TV sets doing Q9 [Spike Milligan's TV series] or whatever was being made at that time, you know? There were some great moments and other bits which looked nice, it was a bit of a waste of film, though.

They weren't talking in damning or mocking tones, it was more slightly pained. The one thing they agree on is that the film was a mess but both seem reluctant to completely dismiss it.

H: I kept thinking it was going to be something different than what it was. It never became anything. The comedy was very broad in places and really funny. And then, sometimes it was like they were just trying to get the plot going.

S: You'd have a sustained few minutes of gag-gag-gag and then the whole film stopped dead again.

H: Some of the gags were SO like... old fashioned.

Hank and Stu got very animated and spent a few minutes comparing moments in Morons to classic gags from The Marx Brothers, Laurel & Hardy and Jacques Tati. For a moment, it feels like they are really singing the film's praises. But they quickly get distracted back towards the negative.

H: That moment where the guy breaks into song to declare his love for the woman?

S: In a hugely developed plot strand that just ends and goes nowhere!

H: And why does he pop up outside Griff Rhys Jones' house dressed as a *Frenchman*? With onions and a beret and a stripy shirt! And he even has a moustache on, it's really weird! There was a lot of it where I thought, when they were on set, they must have looked around a lot and gone "What the fuck are we doing?" it just didn't make any sense at all.

S: There's one bit where its just like a reel went missing, where Griff Rhys Jones goes from being Norman Wisdom to being super-slick-kind-of-guy-dressed-like-Trevor-from-The-Buggles. And then it suddenly becomes this Man Who Fell To Earth thing. Some of the stuff the movie references was really weird considering the humour was pitched young. And what was it satirising? In some ways it feels as if it would work better now, in Trumpland, where everyone's an idiot. The problem here is that they're morons, but everyone on Earth is portrayed as a moron too.

H: Everything was the same – except they called their planet Blob.

S: And the beer was green.

H: But everything else was the same. Oh it was terrible. I mean, they should have had... ugh. Their spaceship was a caravan.

When it started, I just didn't know what was going on. I didn't know if they were humans, I didn't understand. It never made sense that they were aliens, really. Was anyone in it at all likable?

S: Everything with Mel Smith was really grim. Starting with him vomiting in his space helmet!

J: He's sneezing! It's a sneeze!

S: I thought he threw up.

H: His weightless acting was brilliant.

S: But all the Mel Smith lost in America stuff was so grim. It was just like what story are you trying to tell? What story is this?

H: Jimmy Nail was great. He was really well cast. He made some really good faces. He seemed like a good comic actor. He didn't have much to work with, really. He did some good 'waking up from being drunk' acting. The woman was alright. The tall guy didn't seem to have much to do.

S: Well, they're all essentially the same. They're all idiots. If you watch The Three Stooges, each of the Stooges is different. Or The Marx Brothers, you know – usually in this sort of thing, one of them is smart. They're stupid – but everyone in the movie is stupid. They don't seem particularly stupider than anyone else. The politicians are idiots, the American guy is a great fool.

I try to bring some structure to the conversation, perhaps to stymie the total annihilation of all the things I enjoy about this film. I ask them who they think the film was aimed at.

H: I think if I'd seen this in 1985 and I'd been 12, I probably would have really liked it. If I'd seen Griff and Mel… I mean, I'm a little bit old to… if I'd been 11 or 12 and I'd seen them on the telly then seen that, I think I would have really enjoyed it. I've enjoyed much worse films. Comedy films. Around that age.

J: So you think it was for the 12 year old boy market?

H: I think a little older than that. Sort of young teenagers. Maybe a date movie for teenagers cos they go to comedies, don't they? I don't know *who* the fuck it was for.

Hank grabs his forehead and looks distraught. He turns to Stu and asks his opinion.

S: I don't know. I think it was… I think there was something that was intended that was satirical in nature but it just didn't work. I couldn't work out what the real satire was about.

So, it's time for the big question and I'm pretty sure I know what the answer is going to be. I ask them if it was a bad film.

H: I was very worried that it'd be so shit, this film. But it wasn't.

S: What's that terrible Kenny Everett film? Bloodbath in the House of Death? It wasn't as bad as that – that was just garbage. There's a lot of really unwatchable British comedy movies. I would not have been sitting through The Boys in Blue.

H: The funny thing is, it started off well, in the middle I thought "This is going to get bad!" and I got really bored. I thought I was going to fall asleep. I thought the last bit – I wouldn't call it the last act, really, because that's too formal – but the last third, I thought became so scattershot and odd that it became really good. Like they'd given up on the plot. It got better. I was surprised at how much better it got. They put them in that big stadium, and that song the gospel choir was singing was really funny!

S: Well, I would have to admit that it passed the six-laugh test. That's a Kermode thing. It passed the six-laugh test, I wasn't entirely… you know, I… Definitely, there were bits where it was a trudge. Most of the Mel Smith stuff. Although there were a couple of really good gags in there. I liked the whole spaghetti thing. It was worth it for that. If it just turned up on Netflix or something? Would I have made it through to the end? I'm not sure I would have done. But it was quite an enjoyable experience, this evening, watching it.

Neither answered as I had expected, but neither had really answered the question. They seemed to be saying it was not a bad film but it also seemed to be incredibly stressful for each of them to accept this. They both had deeply furrowed brows, were staring at the floor and looked distinctly uncomfortable.

"OK" I say "…so, did you *enjoy* it?"

There is a long pause.

H: Uh……uhhhhh. Yessss. I enjoyed it… I enjoyed it because… I… I mean… If I'd put it on and I'd had a couple of beers and I put it on and it was on Sky, would I keep watching it? I enjoyed it because I wanted to see what you're on about, it was more to do with you than it was… but I think I did enjoy it, actually. I think I did. There were some bits that really made me laugh and I think I would have just about left it on if I got back from a gig or some-thing and put it on at 1am, been drinking, I probably would have watched it all the way through, just as a curiosity because it was so fucked up.

S: There are certain elements of the film, its probably the incompe-tence of the narrative, where you just go "What? What is going on?" totally random things are happening, which gives it a certain, uh, zaniness that has translated into later cultdom for other movies – some of which, I would say, are not very good. That don't really deserve to be reassessed or reappraised, that tends to happen in America, with American films and not so much with British ones. I find myself wondering sometimes that if it had been the same film and had been made in America, would people now be celebrating it?

Stu has slyly avoided answering the actual question directly but he certainly makes a good point. Far worse films are far more celebrated.

So, the verdict seems to be that Morons is a mess of a film, with no clear audience, an abandoned narrative and bizarre attempts at misplaced satire, yet it is a consistently funny and enjoyable film, and in such, hard to completely write-off. I got the feeling that they – Hank more than Stu – had a sort-of fondness for it. They both certainly roared with laughter at various points.

They pointed out things I had never noticed – especially the moment where Matteson breaks into song – he actually does this a couple of times – it is completely unprecedented and destroys the reality the film has established in the same way it would if a character suddenly broke the fourth wall and spoke to camera. I also had not clocked the fact that *every* character in the film is moronic, so how are the rest of them able to elevate the morons to a higher state of moronity?

I feel somewhat vindicated. My fear was that it would just be shit, it seems to be weird enough to exude an indefinable charm. I agree with the consensus that it feels like this film was trying to be something but that the team gave up on that and just went hog-wild. Which is basically just very enjoyable to see.

ARE WE MORONS?

This past bank holiday Sunday, my girlfriend and I went to the pub. It's a good pub. An old pub, a really old pub. Lots of little nooks, lots of old wooden beams and partitions. The kind of place Harvester would eagerly buy, completely knock out all of the internal structure and then build an old-pub-style interior within. It was busy when we got there on Sunday and we ended up getting the table next to *our* table. Sat around *our* table were six young people. It's hard to say how young these days but I'd say they were no younger than 17 and no older than 22. I couldn't help but watch them. Their behaviour fascinated me.

They sat in two groups, each group around a phone. One group was obsessively taking selfies. They would bunch together in a group, take a series of five or six photos, then all hunch over the phone to scrutinize the photos, deciding which to post or whether to re-take. Once posted, they'd all lean in close to the screen and wait for responses. Every online like or comment was hailed, discussed, analyzed. The other group just sat looking at one girl's phone, moving steadily down her Facebook timeline discussing everything they saw there. Maybe this is the modern equivalent of 'Did you see the match last night?' They were clearly interacting – they were all talking and laughing and occasionally screaming but it bore no relation to what I have always seen as pub chats. A chance to shut the outside world out and, in this safe neutral environment, talk either about the heaviest or lightest matters.

Human interaction in it's purest form. Eye contact. Giving your full attention to somebody else.

For a little while, I was sat alone, studying this. They didn't notice me, or perhaps they did notice me and were happy to have an audience. Perhaps not even happy, perhaps they expected an audience, felt entitled to an audience. Nonetheless, I observed. And since my hearing is not great, I really leaned in to do so. One of the girls, it transpires, was trying to take a new photo for her dating app. Over the course of about three minutes, her face flipped through every possible expression from disgust to a sort of Benny Hill-esque resignation in the pursuit of 'alluring'. As she sat there, mugging like a shit 70s comedian into a lump of glass, metal and plastic which had been assembled in a factory in the Far East where they have to suspend nets around the outside of the building to catch suicidal workers, I thought about Morons From Outer Space.

Wikipedia lists 91 incidents in 2016 of people being killed taking selfies. Some of these were ill-advised attempts to take selfies with dangerous animals; many of them were due to taking 'daring' photos in front of moving trains; a substantial amount occurred whilst posing on cliffs or river edges; and the majority of incidents occurring in the U.S. were achieved by citizens posing with loaded guns and accidentally blowing their own heads off. I know there's a popular movement to label this as Darwinism but behind each hilarious guffaw, there's a dead person. A couple of months back, a story did the rounds on social media about a man called Richard Bull who died in the bath after accidentally dropping his IPhone – which was charging at the time. I don't want to hold the man up for mockery, I think it must be impossibly sad for his family and friends to lose him in such a meaningless way. It's just one incident, but his death does have meaning. As a species we are now putting at the very centre of our lives equipment that we know absolutely nothing about. The average person does not know how a smartphone is made, how it works or anything about the inherent dangers it might contain. Perhaps all of this smart, clean technology has also deadened our weariness about potential dangers. Growing up in the 70s and 80s, it felt like we were keenly aware of the ever-looming threat of death surrounding all household appliances. My family actually unplugged the telly every night, less an errant bolt of lightning hit the aerial and explode our wood-panelled magic box. My grandmother's portable heater was a topic of constant anxious discussion due to its highly combustible potential. Most importantly, we knew not to ever, ever take electrical equipment that was plugged into the mains into the bathroom. Indeed, my memories of suicides depicted on TV at that time seemed to mainly be people taking toasters or radios into the bath with them.

Even the inherent danger of cars seems to have changed since then. Back then, a car was a chugging rusty box with metal bits sticking out of it which screeched and growled through the streets, huffing black clouds out the rear exhaust. They looked and sounded dangerous to the pedestrian. Modern cars are all smooth contours and gentle purring engines, they glide through the streets like mercury on silk. They almost make it look like it would be pleasurable to be hit by one at high speed, as if they'd gently whip beneath you, buffing your bottom along the bonnet, windscreen, roof and rear windscreen before gently plopping you back on your feet in their wake.

Modern technology has been simplified and sanitized. Everything is shaped like a nihilist baby toy. Everything has round edges and looks entirely friendly and approachable. A tin opener used to be an exposed jagged metal wheel on a stick, now the whole thing is a soft rubber affair. This plushification of our society could be dangerous. Not knowing the dangers of technology, or not understanding how they even work, makes us vulnerable. Especially as we increasingly rely upon this stuff.

For a while, part of my patter was the contention that nobody should be allowed to use any technology that they couldn't, themselves, build or explain. I stopped saying this when someone correctly pointed out that I, myself, in this order wouldn't even be allowed to use fire. So, I guess I could modify my point to saying that people shouldn't use equipment that they haven't intellectualised. That they haven't stopped to think about. It's a very familiar sight these days to see babies who can't even speak yet sat staring into the abyss of an iPad. Nobody knows yet what the effect of that is or will be on their development. Yet it's now commonplace. They might as well be vaping for all we know about how it will affect them.

In the lifespan of a baby-boomer, the experience of being human has changed exponentially. Before TV, the main extent that technology had pervaded was in manufacture and transport. Even after TV became widespread, how long did people actually spend in front of it – a couple of hours a night? In 2016, a Nielsen report showed that the average American spends ten hours, thirty nine minutes staring into a screen every day. Which is an hour up on their 2015 report.

This could be an incredibly good thing – you'd think that nearly eleven hours a day of constant information might well elevate our species, but we're all in charge of our own curation so it would seem the bulk of people aren't exactly making it a diet of TED talks and Open University coursework. No, the majority of our people are taking in 11 hours a day of cat videos, sub-Agadoo novelty singles, videos of people unboxing things, a massive dollop of far-right lies, celebrity gossip and granny porn. Compare that to previous generations' average 3 or 4 hours in front of the telly having to watch whatever was on – forced diversity of content consumption – where are we headed?

Another question could be 'why are we headed there?' Why are we so surrounded by technology right now? It seems to be gathering apace and inventions which seem, to me, far beyond unnecessary are flooding the market. Last year, Amazon unveiled 'Amazon Dash', a selection of plastic buttons with adhesive backs and product logos on the front. These buttons have wi-fi connectivity. When pressed, the product branded on the button will be immediately placed in your Amazon basket. So, there's an Andrex one which you can mount next to your toilet roll holder. There's an Ariel one you can stick on your washing machine, a Finish one for your dishwasher, a Catsan one for your cat's litter box. There's even a Durex one, which presumably is to be affixed to the midriff or lower back of the person you love. I suppose the Kleenex one is to be attached to your own midriff if you find yourself single. I have no idea how successful Amazon Dash has been but its very existence casts a poor reflection of humankind. That we are now no longer willing or able to either remember or write ourselves a note to buy something as obvious as bog rolls. I remember as a child seeing my mum hoot with laughter that Marks & Spencer were selling crudités in their food department. They were charging three times the price of the vegetables just to have them pre-cut. Of course, now, a large part of the fruit and veg sections in every supermarket is exactly that – pre-cut vegetables. We have somehow become stupid enough to not realize how easy it is to chop. Or perhaps they've fooled us with talk of convenience. It strikes me that modern commerce is driven by convenience. Buttons to order toothpaste, carrot batons, central heating controlled by smartphones, these are things that we don't need in any way and wouldn't have even stopped to think about had we not been told we need them through aggressive marketing.

This year, we have hit the acme of this phenomenon with Amazon Echo. A highly sophisticated bundle of gubbins, all wrapped up in a black cylinder with a glowing LED ring around the top. Inside it waits the artificial intelligence consciousness known as Alexa. Like a cold, dystopian tube of Pringles, she sits quietly in the corner of your room waiting, listening…

To some it clearly sounds seductive, it does your bidding immediately as you ask it to. The six examples offered on the sales page are "Alexa, find me a Chinese restaurant." "Alexa, set a timer for 20 minutes." "Alexa, re-order paper towels." "Alexa, play Katy Perry." "Alexa, what's on my calendar today?" "Alexa, how's my commute?" What is there left to do in this person's life? Consume. Consume. Consume. Don't busy yourself with anything. Just stay in bed, bark your material and factual needs into the ever-listening tube and use your time to watch Amazon TV shows and slowly wank yourself to death. The Amazon delivery guy will be your last point of human contact. And he'll soon be a drone. Which eventually will have a code to open your door. And just hover above you dropping corporate snacks directly down your gullet, past your atrophied jaw.

Commerce drives technology. It always has. So, why don't we have certain technologies available to us? As a species, we have successfully traveled to and returned from space since 1961. 56 years ago. How has the price of this technology not come down? Why have no enterprising entrepreneurs created the domestic civilian spaceship? Why don't we all have them? I don't have the answer to these questions and I'm too lazy to research them, but what I am asking is, could it not be realistic for this technology to have been refined and mass marketed by now? And had it been, could this table of vacuous simpletons I found myself next to in a small pub in North London not, right now, be taking pointless selfies in another galaxy entirely? And were they there and their ship broke down, how equipped would they be to even begin to fix it? And what would that make them?

ARE WE MORONS? PART 2: THE ANSWERS

THE SCIENCE OF MORONS

I started thinking a lot about the science behind Morons From Outer Space. I totally get that not even the writers would have thought about this, but it intrigues me. The film is clearly articulating *something*. So, I wonder how articulate it might actually be. I called upon literally the only scientist I know, Brian Mackenwells, who happens to be the Public Engagement Officer for the Wellcome Trust Centre for Human Genetics. So he should know a thing or two about humans, aliens and, perhaps, moronity. I sent him a DVD of the film and called him up a few days later.

"I enjoyed it immensely!" he tells me affably "It was the sort of film you don't see anymore. Maybe they get made and I don't hear about them, but there's a certain kind-of very British silly anarchy to it which I just haven't seen in years."

"And what about the science?" I ask him.

"Uh, as sci-fi goes, the spaceship stuff, which science-wise, we just throw away. Everyone's allowed to have spaceships, that's fine. But the central question in it is that they look just like us. They're aliens but they look exactly like us, that's the striking thing. And it's pretty smart in how it treats the science in that it just doesn't go into any details and just mines it for jokes. You can kind of… just…i…fy the science they have… in it. The main concept in it that jumped out at me is called Convergent Evolution – I don't know if you've ever heard of that?"

I, of course, hadn't.

"It's the idea that certain sets of traits just appear again and again and again? So, like, the eye has evolved a number of times, sort of independently. Vertebrates, like us, and jellyfish, cephalopods, they all have eyes but our nearest common ancestor was so long ago, we think it maybe had one little area of, like a photoreceptor point? Just a little bit sensitive to basic light, and then they split into these different species and each of them have evolved the exact same eye. More or less. I think cephalopods don't have a blind spot, but the basics – there's a jelly thing, the light hits it, a lens, all of that is basically the same."

He gives me another example.

"OK, echo location – you get that in bats and dolphins – they're not similar creatures to each other but they both evolved the exact same process. A couple of years ago, scientists did something called the Genome Wide Association Study, which is when you take the whole string of DNA from whatever you want to study. Let's say you want to find the DNA associated with eye colour, so you'd get loads of people who were different in lots of different ways, then you look at all of their DNA – you sequence them like a pair and you go "Well, everyone with blue eyes has this exact sequence in this exact place, so this is probably to do with blue eyes – Right?"

"Right"

"And they did that with dolphins and with bats and they found that in 200 different spots, their DNA was exactly the same. And so, up until then they had assumed that because they were so different, there would be a different structure in their DNA to account for echo location – like it might be the same effect but the background machinery would be different, the genes, but it turns out that the background machinery is exactly the same and it just happened to evolve that way. Which kind of suggest that in evolution, there are just engineering solutions that work."

He pauses, clearly expecting me to make some kind of noise to express understanding. I make a kind of uncertain, high-pitched "Mmmmmm". He takes a deep breath and continues.

"The eye evolved that way because it's probably the best way for those things to evolve. It gives you the best bang for your buck. You need two eyes because with one eye you can't judge distance properly. But any more than two eyes, then it requires energy to grow extra eyes but they don't give you any benefit. There's a cost to them. So you end up with most creatures having two eyes. Same with most vertebrates, like us with our skeletons on the inside, we have legs, and so you could argue that the aliens in the film would also look like us because four legs gives you enough mobility to move around but, again, without the evolutionary cost of the extra limbs, and then your front legs are close to your head, so they make sense to start manipulating things with, and so it makes sort of ecological engineering sense to have something with four legs that stands on its back legs and its arms are up here. The things that we do have, there seem to be good reasons for them."

"So, is there a school of thought that if we found aliens they would be humanoid?" I ask him.

"Yeah! Yeah, yeah, yeah, yeah, that's the good answer. It depends what you mean by aliens as well, there are other intelligent creatures, like squids can solve problems at the level of a child. But it's unlikely there'd be an underwater civilization somewhere in the universe that evolves that looks like squid, because you need fire to have tech. You can't get around that. So, they'd have to be ground-dwelling, which means they aren't going to be fishy. They're probably going to be two arms, two legs, stand up straight, two eyes, bi-lateral symmetry, where we're the same left and right, that makes sense as well because we need a back up of most things and we're balanced. So, yeah, there's sort of an argument for that. The argument in astrobiology is that the only example of life we have in the universe of life is our planet, so to make any other guesses would be speculation without any data, so, you know, we should go based on what we see here. But the counter-argument, of course, is that a study with just one example isn't a very good study. We only have one planet, it's not a huge amount of evidence, really. The other idea of science that seems relevant is this idea of Panspermia. It comes from Kelvin, 120 years ago, he suggested it after a volcano explosion in Krakatoa leveled the island, and there was no living things, but they came back a couple of years later and there were new plants. So, they sort of figured that came from seeds flying over on the wind or whatever from other islands. And this gave Kelvin the idea that this is what happened with the earth. Earth comes from some kind of meteorite impact 3.5 billion years ago, and so if we found another species like us out there, there would be an argument that we would share a common ancestor."

"So, the notion that the aliens might be exactly like humans is actually, ironically, quite a clever one?"

"Yeah. There's even an idea that life on Earth potentially came from Mars, because Mars was, a couple of billion years before we were, a watery planet. It had an atmosphere. That's why we keep sending robots up there, because it's potentially interesting, because if you have water, you potentially have life. And there's a theory that if you hit a big rock into Mars, bits of Mars could fly off, bacteria can survive the journey in space, can survive re-entry and can survive landing in a massive explosion. So, life on Earth might have been seeded with life on Mars, because Mars was potentially ahead of us in that way. Which is one of the reasons that they're very paranoid when they send robots up to Mars, to make sure that they're completely clean, because if we find some evidence of life that looks like us in some way, we want to make sure its not because we contaminated it. That would be really important and interesting if we found out that that's where we came from. There's actually a guy in NASA, his job is Planetary Defense Officer. His job is to make sure all the ships are clean and all the robots. 100% sterile. Best job title, Planetary Defense Officer. So, you could argue that the aliens in the movie were following the argument of Panspermia."

"OK. So, I'm wondering then, in the film they look just like us – which seems completely legitimate now – but, culturally, would they have discovered alcohol and clothes and all of that stuff?"

"Well, this is it – it speaks to the earlier stuff about there just being good engineering solutions to things that evolution finds. And there are only a few possible solutions that work, so they keep coming up again and again. Some scientists believe that bits and pieces of our brain evolved, of our social brain, evolved accidental-ly. Around language, particularly, and imagination and all of that stuff, they're all by-products of other survival behaviours that we needed. So, you could sort of say that if they evolved to the point where they were able to make fire, that means their brains would develop in such a way that you'd end up with a society no matter what you do. You end up with individuals, no matter what you do, and therefore you end up with people getting pissed off with each other, no matter what you do, they'll find a way to get drunk. The only example we have of a species that can do that is us, we'll do that with whatever we find, right? Like, if there is a way to get high or drunk or something, someone has found it. Someone has had to try every bark, frog, or whatever, just on the off-chance that it'd make them high. So you have to assume that'd be true everywhere. We're not special."

"But is that even true of other species on *this* planet?"

"You do find animals that get fruit that falls and ferments and they get a bit drunk and they'll know that can happen and seek it out – I think there's a species of monkey that knows that they'll sort of get drunk if they seek it out. Yeah, it may be associated with intelligence in some way – we experiment to make things more fun and getting drunk is part of that stuff."

Now we're talking about human evolution, we're getting close to the ideas that inspired me to call him in the first place.

"When you compare regular, consumer life in 1985 to today," I start, in my most desperately intelligent tone of voice, "We're in a much more technological society. We have advanced, just in that time –, in a lot of ways we've advanced much further than what was detailed in sci-fi of that time. On an everyday level. Right now, we have people getting demonstrably stupider, in a sense, because politically education and access to education is waning, we are seeing a certain dumbing-down of society, and yet consumer technology is advancing, so we're getting it into the hands of people who don't understand how it works and yet are incorporating it into their lives anyway, people are spending a lot more time looking at screens, we're seeing people taking selfies and falling off cliffs. Is there something about the speed of technological advance in relation to the speed of evolution of a species?"

"It's difficult to say. In terms of speed of evolution, we're not entirely sure how fast evolution works. There's the idea that evolution is constantly happening and that there are random evolutionary mutations all of the time, so the species is always changing a little bit all of the time. The idea that technology has removed that slightly from us, because it's a friction where species would become better, or faster, or smarter, more fit – as in how hard it is to survive or reproduce. We have technology now to protect us from all of that, so we don't really have as many evolutionary pressures on us. So, we might be hitting a slightly flat bit of evolution, potentially. We don't know that for sure because evolution is just people deciding who to have sex with, people are making decisions on who to have sex with, so there will still be some evolutionary pressure. People aren't dying because of hard winters anymore. Except because of the Tories. So, there's this idea that technology had buffered us from forces of evolution and we're not sure, because there's this other idea with evolution that it doesn't just constantly happen, but that you get these periods of stability, where a species stays more or less the same until something happens, like a volcano explodes or the climate changes. But the two camps don't really like each other – the constant change evolution camp and the 'it happens in fits and starts' camp. They have nicknames for each other! When they brought along this 'Stable Evolution' idea, they called it 'Evolution By Jerks' and then they called the other side 'Evolution By Creeps'! Scientists are good at very many things, but not so good at trash talk. So, maybe species are mostly stable until something happens, maybe that's happening now with technology, so maybe there'll be some kind of accelerated evolution as a result of this new pressure or maybe not – maybe we're protecting ourselves from the actual evolutionary pressure. We don't know and it hasn't been around long enough for us to say, it's only been twenty or thirty years, one generation."

"In terms of the universe, how intelligent are we?"

"That also speaks to the idea "what does intelligence mean?", as far as we know, we're the only ones out here, which probably makes us quite special, but you know SETI (Search For Extraterrestrial Intelligence)? They have been looking for maybe 50 or 60 years and they haven't really found anything. But they've only searched maybe 1% of possible frequencies in a tiny corner of the entire sky. It could be that alien civilizations are out there but they're just using frequencies that we don't. Using some other system, maybe they do all their TV through gravitational waves or something we haven't figured out yet. But, as far as we know, we are the only ones that are intelligent, going by our definition of intelligence.

"Do you think that if we were to go out into the universe and find other civilizations, would we be the morons? How would we appear? Sci-fi's job is to relate reality back to us, so is that what the filmmakers might have been doing? Saying that if we went out into space, we would also be the morons?"

"Particularly because, you'll see that NASA send the best and brightest into space, but in the film it's certainly implied that space travel is a completely normal thing – they're *renting* a spaceship! So, it's just that normal people have access to space travel. So, yeah, if we went out there – just normal people – well, we're not going to cover ourselves with glory. There's no way we wouldn't be the morons. Particularly, if like in the film, a spaceship landed, we'd assume they're better than us because they can pilot spaceships, but we'd only let other alien civilizations down, really."

"OK, exactly, so, the one single thing these four morons have above humankind on Earth is the ability of interplanetary travel. Why don't we have that?"

"Because it's really hard. Basically, it's just the distances involved. To get enough speed to get anywhere within human lifetimes, it's just too many problems to get around. You have to reinvent fuel. One of the problems they have with rockets is that in order to get enough energy to get off a planet, you need fuel. But the more weight you have, the more fuel you need, so you put more fuel in, you increase the weight, so then you need fuel to push the fuel that you just put in. So, that's why it's so expensive to go to space. It takes a ton of fuel to get off the planet and we don't have any better ways to do that other than blowing things up at the moment. And, once you're up there, there are things like Solar Sails. The probe that went past Pluto – it had very small nuclear motors that just give it a very, very gentle push – so they can go very very slowly but they go for a very long time. So we can traverse distances that way but, then, you need to freeze people or you need to do Generation Ships, where everyone lives on the ship for generations to get to their goal planet. And space is also just really hostile. So protecting people that are up there is very hard, even coming within about a million miles of Jupiter, Jupiter's still cooling down from when the solar system was formed, so it's still giving off a ton of radiation. That will kill people. So you need a heavy amount of shielding, which makes the whole thing heavier, which makes it more expensive to put into space and so on. There's no technical reason, it's just very hard, which makes it very expensive. To do it in the way that they're doing it in the film, that implies a faster-than-light travel and, as far as we can tell, that's impossible. Because one of the things that Einstein proved is that you can't go faster than the speed of light. It's basically because, when you go through the equations, you need infinite energy to hit that point, to go faster than that. And the equation just breaks, you end up with a zero at the bottom of division sign, in the equation that we've discovered describes the universe quite accurately. So, yeah, you just need an infinite amount of energy, so we can't go faster than the speed of light. There's all sorts of sci-fi ideas about black holes and doing the classic thing where instead of going in a line, bend space so you go through – but that's the only idea we have of traversing large distances, is to somehow cheat."

"But that's not in any way proven?"

"No. No, it might be possible, depending on how you look at the equations. We know space ends, already, just because that's how all the planets are in their orbits. The sun is like a big heavy lead ball on a rubber sheet that bends space, and all the planets are spinning around on the edge of this, with enough sideways speed that they stay in the same spot and the same distance. So we do know space bends, and if we could figure out how to do that, we might be able to punch through the other side. But it's all just theory and speculation and some clever equations. All the ways we have to travel distances involves just pushing ourselves and that takes a long time and has a speed limit anyway. Even if you could go at the speed of light, the distances are so vast that the nearest star is Proxima Centauri, which probably has planets, and that would still take you 40 or 50 years. Space is just too big."

"So, is the theory that we couldn't be visited by aliens?"

"Yeah, you can't prove a negative, I guess, maybe – in theory – you can do something with space where it bends or some mechanism that we haven't discovered, or maybe relativity goes funny when you go at very high speeds and it all breaks, who knows? But nobody can figure out a way for it to happen. I think there's reasonably wide acceptance in science that there probably is aliens, and maybe even intelligence, but they're just very far away. There's something called the Drake Equation. Have you ever heard of that?"

Of course I've never heard of that. I failed GCSE Science.

"It's this idea, a way to calculate how much intelligent life, how many civilizations there might be in the galaxy. Or in the universe. The idea is that you take how many stars there are, then you take away all the stars that don't have planets and you're left with a smaller number, and you take away all the stars that have planets but the planets aren't in the right place or the right size to have water. We think you need water to have life. Because that allows all the molecules to move around in such a way as to create complex molecules. Again, the only example we have is Earth, but we needed water to have life. So, you're left with the planets that have water on them, and then you take away the ones that might have life, and then you work out the probability of those that are left that might have intelligent life, and then you work out the probability of those that have intelligent life that could communicate to us, and then you take the number of whatever the probability is of those that can communicate to us that are still around and haven't destroyed themselves, and you're sort of left with a final number of an estimate. And you can get quite informed with all of those estimates, you can make reasonably informed guesses of the probability of intelligent life and the probability of life occurring based on all sorts of maths I don't understand. But the problem is that the estimates using the Drake Equation vary from a hundred million civilizations in our galaxy alone or zero. Depending on how optimistic or pessimistic your instructions are about all sorts of aspects about it.

The most depressing thought, however, is that maybe civilizations appear all over the place but they naturally implode after a few thousand years. Eventually, a nuclear bomb will happen. Maybe every civilization makes a nuclear bomb eventually, maybe once it's there eventually someone uses it and eventually it all just implodes. Like, it's inevitable."

So, what Brian might essentially be saying here is that maybe everyone, all intelligent life throughout the entire universe, can only get to a certain point of evolution before we push the big red button and wipe ourselves out. That, just perhaps, all intelligent life could ultimately be defined as Morons From Outer Space.

I ask him if anything else struck him from the film.

"The scientists who opened the spaceship had very sloppy safety protocols. Very bad PPE – Personal Protective Equipment. Because they're all wearing helmets and then they took them off once they'd been through the thing that squirted them, the washing machine thing. I wrote it down. Our health and safety officer would go mad. You have to keep all that stuff on, so that you're completely sure that there isn't alien bugs or whatever! Otherwise, just leave it off entirely. I wrote that down."

He chuckles as he winds down a bit.

"One last thing – and this is just because of my job, it made me laugh particularly, remember when they're being interviewed by the scientists? And she's like "Oh, you know this song, don't you? You know the song, Tempt Me Sideways" and she starts singing it – and it's an alien planet!!! It made me think about how scientists talk about science. They're from a different planet from everyone else, they're in this world where technical information is known very widely and everyone understands that GWAS means Genome Wide Association Study or whatever. And so they say "Oh, you know this one, don't you? You know! The Drake Equation! You know this one!" The way the aliens were talking reminded me of how scientists talk to the public."

HOW FAR IS TOO FAR?

I'm not sure how many famous cats there are. And mine certainly isn't known, but he has a unique claim to fame. When I first set up my film production company – which was a hasty affair, necessitated by certain legal demands – I had to come up with a name very quickly during a phone call to my accountant. I looked around for inspiration and saw the cat sat on the windowsill looking out at the canal. "Canal Cat Films". While finishing up Elstree 1976, Hank and I realised that all of the other companies involved in the production had cool animated logos for the opening. So we commissioned our illustrator pal Dan Mumford (who also played George Lucas in the recreation scenes) to design a logo – with my cat's face in the middle of it. Then we got our animator pal Kris Martin to animate it. This means that the cat has appeared on cinema screens from Portsmouth to Tokyo, he has been seen in every continent on the planet. He has popped up on TV screens right across America since the film appeared on Netflix and Britain since its Sky premiere. Not confined by earthly concerns, he has also been seen many of thousands of feet into the heavens thanks to Qantas buying the airplane rights.

But the cat is unwell. For eleven years he has been my bizarre companion. My furry flatmate. My unwanted 4am land-on-your-chest-so-hard-it-might-be-a-heart-attack wake-up call. A few weeks ago, he started to withdraw and spent most of each day under the bed. Whenever he came out, he would drink water with ferocious speed, drinking almost ten times his usual amount. The vet told us he was diabetic. The hospitalisation was costly, the tests were costly, the treatment was costly. I had not bought insurance. My finances tumbled fast. I was worried but never once thought about not putting his treatment first. Within a few weeks, I was cleaned out and into my overdraft for the first time in a few years.

Having a diabetic cat is not the easiest situation. You have to learn how to give injections and then you have to administer those injections twice a day at 8am and 8pm directly after the cat has eaten. Along with this, the cat is restricted to one single type of food. A special medical food. I'm not sure what is special about it other than the cost. Which is *incredibly* special. Cats are fiercely independent animals and the unholy trifecta of trying to get this one to, firstly, eat the horrible food, secondly, do so at eight on the dot and, thirdly, allow me to give him an injection right afterwards was fast becoming the main focus of my life. It had eclipsed the previous focus of my life which was my upcoming wedding. The wedding being the exciting and happy focus, but both were a bit stressful. So, I needed a project for a measure of distraction. This book. I thought it might be fun. But then I realized that Morons From Outer Space had become the third focus of my life.

It had shifted out of the lifelong realm of comfort viewing on a winter's afternoon when laid up with the flu and transformed into obsession. I'm no stranger to obsession, it has always been a motivating force in my life. It began with Star Wars when I was five and moved through many iterations – Transformers, Tootsie, Psycho 2, Highlander, The Blues Brothers, the 1989 Batman film, into music – The Cure, The Levellers, KISS, Cheap Trick, and then back to film in a more general way in my adulthood. My obsessions are smaller and more contained now, but still quite… obsessive. It begins with immersing myself in watching the film, or films, a little too much, then buying and reading every book on the subject, then getting some significant memorabilia associated with it and culminates in the need to OWN a piece of it. The most recent one was a rediscovery of Charlie Chaplin. I'd watched Attenborough's rather great biopic, starring Robert Downey Jr, then started re-watching all of the Chaplin films, then the shorts, then I read a biography, then I read his autobiography, then I dropped over a hundred quid on the massive, beautiful Charlie Chaplin Archives book by Taschen which weighs about a ton and comes in a huge cardboard box with a carry handle. Inside the book, exclusive to the first print run, is a strip of 12 frames from a 35mm print of City Lights direct from the Charlie Chaplin Archives. A beautiful object in a beautiful object in a beautiful box. I went out and bought a special table just to house it. But it wasn't enough. I wanted a PIECE of Chaplin. It's not all that hard to find a Charlie Chaplin autograph. He was the most famous man in the world for a while. He spent a lot of time signing autographs and those autographs were rarely thrown away. But they're expensive and, really, without serious provenance, you'd never really know, would you? Memorabilia exists, old film posters, that sort of thing. But it's all so expensive. So, as I've done before, I find myself dedicating more and more time to scouring eBay and websites of auction houses looking for something meaningful and affordable. I strike partial-gold. One of my lifelong heroes has been film poster artist Drew Struzan. Notoriously withdrawn, until quite recently, I had longed for his autograph – his autograph being famous in itself. If you look at any big budget Hollywood film poster from the 70s or 80s, you have a good chance of spotting a 'DREW' on there somewhere. I found out that, for an exhibition of his work in California, Drew signed a pile of lithographs of his Charlie Chaplin portrait. I scored one. Two birds, one stone. Except, no, obsession doesn't work that way. It's a piece of Drew, it's a picture of Chaplin, it's still not a piece of Chaplin.

Eventually, I find out about Panini's Americana. Americana is a series of trading cards which seem to be about famous Americans.

The set itself is a gaudy collection of what look like very cheaply licensed candid photos of the stars but what sets this series apart is the generous distribution of randomly inserted 'chase' cards. Many of these are autographed – in this series alone, you had the very real possibility of securing yourself the squiggle of anyone from Larry Hagman to Brigitte Nielsen although, really, what would you do with either? But then, they came up with a bit of a stroke of genius. Swatch cards. They bought up well-provenanced personal clothing from Hollywood legends, cut these items into ½ inch square swatches and incorporated them into special cards. There is a school of thought that what they have actually done is destroy a historical artifact but, I think, it's quite wonderful – it gives a lot of people a chance of owning a tiny piece of something significant to them. Their remit spread right across Hollywood history and, sure enough, they had produced a Chaplin card. It cost me about £15. It sated my obsession upon arrival. And there it sits on my shelf, a square ½ inch of soft black linen with a delicate silver pinstripe. A little piece of Chaplin, in my life. On my shelf. My next obsession was Errol Flynn. Again, sated by a swatch card. Hank has always been obsessed with Orson Welles, so I bought him an Orson one as a present.

"That's amazing! Thank you!"
"You're very welcome, man!"
"What piece of clothing is it from?"

We both lean in and scrutinise it. It's just black material.

"Probably his pants" I conclude.
"Yes" frowns Hank "I'll treasure it always."

Over the years, I've amassed a collection of film memorabilia – nothing hugely expensive – although, usually on the outer-edge of affordable to me at the time of purchase, but small and significant and kind of cool. Aside from the novelization, I own nothing of Morons From Outer Space. And I feel the thirst rising.

A couple of years ago, I worked on a short documentary about the big annual film prop and costume auction that takes place in London every year. One of the lots up for auction was the character Leeloo's Multi Pass from the film The Fifth Element. The catalogue estimate for this prop – admittedly, a key prop but essentially a fake driving licence with a button glued on to it – was £4k – 6k. "Nobody is going to pay that!" I confidently proclaimed "It's not that big of a film!" While our cameras rolled, a couple from somewhere in Mid-West America paid £35k for it. And seemed quite happy to have done so. Using rough arithmetic, comparing the box office take and enduring popularity of The Fifth Element to Morons, I calculated that I could pick up a key prop from my film of choice – perhaps the model of their space-ship or Des's 'LOOB' baseball cap – for less than £3.50.

I'd got friendly with Stephen Lane the twinkly-eyed CEO of Propstore – the company who run the auction and the world's biggest film prop/costume sales website – and decided to email him to see if he could help me maximise my £3.50 investment in Morons props. The film prop market is a massive one and pretty much anything that has appeared onscreen in any capacity has considerable value now. Wandering the aisles of Stephen's massive warehouse, you'll find everything from 007's jet boat from the opening of The World is Not Enough to a shelf full of pots of arrows. Although looking basically the same, the untrained eye seeing an arrow as an arrow and little more, there was a great variance in the value of these arrows. An arrow from Ridley Scott's dull 2010 telling of the Robin Hood story would set you back just £15. An arrow from The Last Samurai? £35. It's a better film, isn't it? A Gyptian arrow from The Golden Compass will set you back £45, if you want a Witch's arrow from the same not-very-

good-but-isn't-it-nice-to-see-Sam-Elliot-get-a-decent-payday? –
film £95. £75 will get you an arrow from the stoner comedy Your
Highness. It's apparently the type fired throughout the film by
Natalie Portman. It has no arrowhead, though. For safety purposes. £145 will get you a 'bloody' SFX arrow from Sin City, but the
crème de la crème is a pair of arrows from The Brothers Grimm,
belonging to Lena Heady's character – £195 the pair. I know. For
sticks. I'm left wondering who is ever going to buy those. Who
cares about The Brothers Grimm? It was a lesser Gilliam film. I
could imagine if it were a prop that Heath Ledger had touched, it
would be worth some money but I'd have thought this falls very
much into the 'stick it in a skip at the end of shooting because,
honestly, who cares?' category. But what do I know? Following
this logic, surely – surely – in some warehouse, somewhere, are a
bunch of props from Morons From Outer Space that somebody
thinks has saleable value but everybody else in the world disagrees. Except me and my £3.50.

Stephen swiftly replied to my email:

Hey Jon,

Good to hear from you.

*I'm sorry to say that very, very little turns up from this movie.
I'm not sure that I've seen more than a couple of pieces in my 25
years of collecting.*

Sorry that I can't be more positive on this occasion!

Stephen

So I decided to do what Stephen had told me he did when he
started collecting Star Wars props and costumes several decades
earlier – to get in touch with people who had worked on the film
and see if they had kept hold of anything they might be willing to
part with. A bit of research revealed that, really, a lot of people
involved with the film are either dead or Jimmy Nail. I can't

imagine the response I'd get from Jimmy Nail if I contacted him asking for memorabilia from literally his least iconic film performance. I had visions of his massive face crumpling into a look of weary disdain.

The obvious points of contact were the production design team, the FX team and the costume department. The production designer and the costume designer had been married – Bryan Ealwell and May Routh. Bryan had sadly died but May was listed as lecturing at a university in the US. I sent her a polite email asking if she might have any of her – or her late husband's – work from this film that she might like to sell. She did not respond. I tore through the credits list on IMDB and couldn't find contacts for all but one of the still-breathing production team of Morons. I emailed him – an uncredited set designer from the art department. He responded jovially that he had fond memories of that shoot but that he currently lived in the US and any work he had left over – probably a sketch or two – would be in storage somewhere in the UK.

One day I found myself stood next to Griff Rhys Jones on the Northern Line platform at Tottenham Court Road Station. Just stood next to him. If there is a God, he was having a lunchtime giggle, throwing some kind of test my way. I had a minute until the train arrived. He's just stood there. Next to me. Do I turn to him and say "Hello Griff, you don't know me, but I'm writing a book specifically about the one thing you have done in your long career which has been most reviled by critics and audiences". Maybe I do. What do I have to lose? What *did* I have to lose? Well, what I had to lose is the chance to do this through the appropriate channels. It goes wrong and when I finally do put a request in with his agent, the response will be 'No, and stop harassing him in public places.' So we just stood there. But then I had another thought. What if I were to approach him as a collector?

"Griff," I did not say, "I know it's a bit random, but I'm a collector of film memorabilia. Would you have any props or interesting memorabilia left over from Morons From Outer Space?" But then I realized… what if he said "Yes'? What if he'd offered me the iconic 'sneeze' helmet from the film and named his price at a thousand pounds? I wouldn't have been able to say no. I'm no longer in that part of my life where I'm free from responsibility and could blow my cash on whatever. I'm still paying for the cat's injections. But, then, what if he said "Yes, I've got a big box of Morons crap in the shed and you'd be doing me a favour to get rid of it"? What to do? What to do? I, of course, did nothing – to talk to him would have been INSANE. So I walked away from him and stood thirty feet down the empty platform.

Every day, at some point, I check EBay to see if anything might come up unexpectedly – I've made incredible scores through random searches before. A Japanese press book appears for a tenner and I buy it without even thinking. When it arrives, it's a thing of wonder. A beautiful, glossy programme full of great photos and very exciting-looking text. The centre spread is… strange. A big piece of 'art' made up of doodles, paint and a collage of cut-up photos, seemingly by a troubled mind. A photo of Mel Smith inexplicably has a grinning mouth placed on his forehead. Griff's head is on a spoon being eaten by the burly man from the diner in the film. A half-length photo of Sandra is completed with crayons, giving her an outsized bottom. It's nice to own, but it's still hardly a one-of-a-kind.

I'm signed up to the mailing list of a slew of online auction houses. Places which do big auctions of film memorabilia, the likes of which I could never afford but I enjoy perusing the catalogues greatly. One day a link to an online catalogue of an online poster auction arrives in my inbox. As I digitally paw through it, I see the word 'Morons'. On offer, with an expected value of £150 – £250 are two prototype poster designs for Morons. This is the first time I've ever seen any one-of-a-kind Morons item. It has to be said, you can see why these concepts were rejected. The first is horrible. Big, ugly cartoonish lettering. Covered in rubbish gags like 'Special effects by Plastickits-on-strings ltd' and 'filmed entirely in Stomachchurnaround' and 'warning: special effects so distracting that you'll eat your hankie and blow your nose on your choc-ice!' The second, I rather like. A painting of a caravan floating in space with the film's title in the style of the Star Wars opening crawl. I read the description and realize that there is another dimension to these: they're from the archive of Vic Fair, probably Britain's most famous film poster artist. And these are hand drawn and painted by him. I curse myself. Why is this special to me? I can call Vic Fair legendary but he's only legendary to, like, twenty people, of which I'm one. He's not legendary. He was a jobbing artist. But he did some iconic work. He did the beautiful artwork for the posters of The Man Who Fell To Earth, Baron Munchausen, the less beautiful artwork for all of the Confessions films. I shouldn't care. I shouldn't buy these. But I sign up for the auction. I have regrets. In the past, I've let things go and regretted it later. I could have bought the original blueprints for the shark from Jaws for a fairly affordable price. I could have bought a full set of Colonial Marines dog tags from Aliens, back before film props became big business. For the next 24 hours, I put bids in and then retract them. Is £150 reasonable? For two original Vic Fair pieces of art? For 2 one-of-a-kind Morons items? For a man who is in his overdraft? Yesterday, a trip to the vets had cost over £300. If money is flying out of the door so arbitrarily, why not an extra £150? And does this count as an investment? Is there anyone in the world who would ever pay as much as me for this lot? And what happens to all of this stuff when I die? Am I just filling the attic with crap which my poor wife and children will have to spend time working out what the hell it is and sending it back to the auction houses it came from to pay off my debts? If I win these things, what will I even do with them? I don't have any wall space in my study and it wouldn't be fair to display them anywhere my long-suffering fiancée would have to see them. Why do I want these fucking things? Why do I care?

The only answer to that question that has ever rung true with me was from Paul Blake, who played Greedo in Star Wars. When I asked him why people want autographs, he told me that he had thought about that quite a lot and what he had come up with was that we appreciate film as an art form but that film is frustratingly ephemeral. A film is not a tangible, physical *thing*. When you own a painting, you can see the brushstrokes. A painting is a physical remnant from an artistic act and when that act was concluded, the artist signed it. He suggested that getting an autograph from the people who creatively contributed to the art of a film was perhaps a moment of closure or completion for the person who loved that film and a tangible physical object they can possess. Where is the remnant with film, though? The thing that was *there* as the art happened. The original camera negative? The lens the light passed through? The camera which closed the gate on it? I did once see one of the cameras Star Wars was filmed on sell for a lot of money at auction. Where is it? Where is the artistic moment preserved? For me, objects have power, to own a thing that was *there* that was in the room, that has meaning. Even if it's half a square inch of Orson Welles' massive y-fronts.

I log in to the online auction. My lot number is 376. I was born in '76. I take this as a hugely meaningful sign. Although, in the same auction lots 76 (25 British quad film posters including The Sea Wolves and Risky Business), 176 (two Japanese Shaft posters) and 276 (quad posters for tepid Britpop doc Live Forever and The Filth and the Fury) seem curiously less meaningful. Still, 376. Yes. This lot must be destined to be mine.

The live webcast begins. A young Irish guy sat with a gavel makes light work of tearing through the lots. A beautiful original poster for The Ladykillers goes for £520. A poster for The Shining goes for £60, which seems like a bargain. Even getting through a lot per minute, I know it'll be several hours to go until 376. An original Mad Max poster gets £160, Blade Runner just £120. A Jaws one-sheet poster makes £300. On we go, on we go. A lot of 3000 unspecified 'modern' film posters goes for just £40. There is laughter in the room. They must be real crap. The Great Escape poster hits £1500.

A couple of hours pass, a new auctioneer comes in. A bald man with a poor attempt at a comb-over who is not afforded dignity by the camera angle. The Vic Fair lots start coming up. The poster proofs are not selling high. Below estimate, in fact. Perhaps I'll get lucky. The cat wanders in and rolls over at my feet. Yesterday, he was declared fit again. It turns out a cat can recover from diabetes within a month. My bank account is unlikely to recover so quickly. Especially if I win this. I'm wondering why the cat came in right now, minutes before my lot. Is he encouraging me or trying to tell me that he might get expensive again some time soon? I can see my lot creeping up the screen. 373. 374. 375.

Then a strange thing happens. The auctioneer seems to want to get through lot 376 quickly. He doesn't name or describe it. He starts the bidding at the lowest estimate £150. When nobody bids that, instead of lowering the price, he just passes on the whole lot. Truthfully, as I see what he's doing, I click the 'bid £150' button but, thankfully I'm too late. I mean, that would have been too much money. £80 would have been too much, but I'd have paid it. I'm left with a mixture of frustration and utter relief. I realize that the only two possible outcomes would have been disappointment or buyer's remorse, so why do I continue to put myself on this merry-go-round? Whenever I get a piece of film memorabilia which has great meaning to me, I go through the same process. I can't wait for it to arrive. Then, when it does arrive, I stare at the unopened box for a while. So excited. Then I open it and marvel at the contents. For a week, I will find myself staring at the object in every idle moment. Not quite believing that this piece of cinema history is mine. Is in the same room as me. Then I'll become accustomed to it. Then I won't notice it anymore. But then, one day, I *will* notice it again. And it will give me delight again. And, that's what it's all about. It's about delight.

The night after the auction, I take my girlfriend out to dinner and I get the bill – which has been an embarrassing rarity recently since the financial problems, but I reason that if I had been prepared to drop £80 on two Morons artifacts, then that unspent money should go on a meal with the woman I love. We had sushi. It was great. It came to £50. Meals out in London usually come to at least £50. And then it struck me; if it's acceptable to drop that much on something that will be enjoyed for half an hour and then literally flushed down the toilet, why am I feeling guilty about spending that kind of money or something which will provide me delight for at least twice as long?

Film obsession. I think for most film obsessives, the behaviour goes unchecked. They don't stop to question it. They just allow their lives to be slowly taken over by it. I question everything. To me, the concept of an unexamined life sounds like a dream holiday. Sometimes film feels like a burden to me, a distant god demanding constant worship and offering but the thing is, if you find something that provides you with delight, it's not a bad thing to indulge. Even if that thing is Morons From Outer Space. And maybe, just maybe, one day I might get to own that helmet.

NICE HELMET

Let's talk about the helmet. Arguably, the most iconic moment – iconic, might be the wrong word – let's say *memorable*... Arguably the most *memorable* moment in this film is Mel Smith's beautifully performed space helmet sneeze. At that point in time, almost 90 years of cinematic science fiction had managed to accrue without anybody considering what might happen if you were to sneeze in one of those things. It's a brilliant moment. In all, Mel spends just a couple of minutes, a couple of sequences, in his spacesuit, yet that image of him looking slightly grumpy in that helmet is the image on the film's posters and advertising.

To me, the space helmet *was* iconic. It seemed bigger than the usual type you'd see in films or even in NASA footage. By the time I was a teenager, I realised that the helmet was actually, probably, some form of satire. It was clearly designed to ape the helmets worn by the crew of the Nostromo from Alien, with the nubbin on top, the wide, bowled glass front surrounded by technonubbery and hoses leading to a backpack.

But then, maybe it wasn't satire – there was nothing intrinsically funny about it. Although it can, admittedly, be hard with this film to work out which things are supposed to be funny. Maybe they'd just ripped the design off from Alien costume designer John Mollo – also the costume designer of Star Wars. It turns out that the truth is neither satire nor theft.

It's not theft because the Morons spacesuit was designed by John Mollo. So, why isn't he credited as costume designer on the film? Well, it's a slightly disappointing story. One of those stories which just robs cinema of all of its magic and reminds you what a cynical affair film production is.

Mollo, having won the 1978 Oscar for Costume Design on Star Wars and the 1979 BAFTA for the same on Alien seems to have slightly, perhaps, rested on his laurels for his next foray into sci-fi. Outland is a well-respected, if slightly forgotten, Sci-fi thriller from 1981. It's really good, you should check it out. It was Sean Connery's return to the genre after 1974's bat-shit crazy Zardoz in which he, famously, wears just an orange nappy-and-suspenders combo throughout. Outland finds him somewhat more appropri- ately clothed and he spends some of the film wearing a helmet which looks suspiciously like the ones in Alien. Gone are the big bulky suits themselves, in favour of lighter canvas jumpsuits, but the helmets worn by Connery and much of his fellow cast are pretty darn similar, although not identical.

If you're prepared to delve into the dark part of the internet (oh, Jesus, no, not *that* dark part) you'll find forums inhabited by film prop collectors and worse... replica prop builders... who will discuss such matters at length. On the boards at propsummit.com (summit!), which is primarily a resource for fans of Blade Runner prop discussion (sample thread title: 'Roy Batty Coat Buttons'), I find a thread devoted to the Outland spacesuits. This thread is the very definition of the phrase 'Too Much Information'. In just a few short minutes I not only know what the greeblies on the helmet are, I also know what the word 'greeblies' means. Nobody should know what 'greeblies' means. Join me in my hell. Greeblies are just little bits of wood or plastic that prop builders glue onto space- ships or spacesuits or any other space-things to make them look more complex. They just add texture and look all technical. If you think about the surface of the Death Star in Star Wars – that's basically 100% greeb. The thread went so far as to reveal what the actual greeblies specifically are – it features photos of DIY supplies from the late 1970s and identifies them. The exact ventilation fan cover on the helmet is revealed to be a WELPAC brand Ventilator, model number 8256. The purveyor of this information has even figured out that the distinctive sun-looking design on the nubbin at the top of the helmet is an imprint from the back of the ventilator piece. This board member had, at some point, borrowed one of these helmets and made extensive notes and documentation on them. The helmets were plastic vac-formed, which is a process which allows many cheap, identical helmets to be produced from one master. The helmets were fabricated by a man called Andrew Ainsworth.

Ainsworth is famous in Star Wars fan circles as the man who made the Stormtrooper armour. He's perhaps more famous in the wider world as the David to George Lucas's Goliath. It turns out that there is somewhat of a grey area when it comes to actual film props. Not replicas, you'll need to keep up.

Ainsworth was a young plastic vac-former based in Twickenham when Star Wars came knocking. Kayaks and fishponds were his stock in trade. Ainsworth's friend Nick Pemberton had been hired to fashion the Stormtrooper helmets by Lucas himself. Lucas approved Pemberton's concept sculpture and Ainsworth was given the go-ahead to create moulds for mass production. Ainsworth sculpted the moulds by hand using Pemberton's clay head as a visual reference.

Ainsworth kicked around the UK film industry for a few years following Star Wars and provided his services for films such as Alien, Superman, Flash Gordon and – hey – Outland. Back to that shortly. First we have to skip forward a couple of decades. Ainsworth had left the film industry and was making a living producing watersports equipment. In need of a few bob for his kids school fees, he found an old Stormtrooper helmet in a cupboard somewhere and whacked it into a film memorabilia auction at Christies. It went for 60k. Learning quickly about the burgeoning Star Wars fan scene, he dusted off the old Stormtrooper moulds and started making authentic helmets and armour for the rabid fan base.

Learning about what seemed like a massive copyright infringement, Lucas launched a $20m lawsuit against Ainsworth to shut the operation down, arguing that he did not hold the Intellectual Property rights. The US courts agreed but since Ainsworth had no assets over there, Lucas's lawyers started a case in the UK. The crux of the case was whether the Stormtrooper armour could be classified as a work of art – in which case, the copyright would be owned by the author for his lifetime plus 70 years – or if it counted as 'industrial props' which would give Lucas only a 15 year copyright over it, which would have expired in the early 90s. It went through the whole British court system with both the High Court and the Court of Appeal ruling in Ainsworth's favour – meaning you can now buy a Stormtrooper helmet direct from the man who made them.

Ainsworth was always confident in his case because, for whatever reason, that is how film props apparently are treated in this country. The person who builds them owns them and, when the film is finished, they can do what they want with them. Including renting them out for other projects. So, in a roundabout way, you can perhaps now see that if a British Sci-Fi comedy with a modest budget and not looking to win any Costume Design Oscars might be looking for a space helmet, they might come knocking on Ainsworth's door. And he might have a shedload of leftovers from Outland.

The helmet and backpack that both Mel and Jimmy Nail (in the opening sequence) wear in Morons are direct from Outland. When you compare the two films you'll notice a stark difference. Connery's helmet is filled with little LED lights which give him a real film-star glow, whereas Mel seems to be lit from a standard bulb on the helmet's ceiling. Also, the bright clean side lights of Outland are replaced by one red and one green bulb for Morons. The change is not surprising. Back then, film props were not treated as future museum pieces. When Outland finished, the costumes would have been stripped of bulbs and battery packs to be used in other subsequent projects.

As one does, I got sucked deeper into this story and found a rather delightful blog called 'Say Hello Spaceman' by a chap called Steve Prideaux who just chronicles whenever he sees people in classic style fishbowl space-helmets. Since this is his field of expertise, he has become rather good at spotting when certain helmets resurface. The Outland helmets, it would be fair to say, are pretty ubiquitous. Besides Morons, they can be seen in such wildly varying productions as shoddy Brigitte Nielsen TV movie Murder by Moonlight and James Cameron's masterpiece Aliens – in which they are worn by the deep space salvage team who discover Ripley. Perhaps most magnificently, the helmets were used in the first couple of series of Red Dwarf. That shot at the beginning of every show where Lister is outside painting the spaceship? That's what he's wearing.

To me, this highlights one of the sadnesses experienced when a film fan takes a look behind the curtain. We like to think that the films we hold dear to us were as dear to the people who made them and it's a little disappointing to learn that the things we see on that screen were maybe not lovingly crafted for us but cheaply sourced and thrown together.

So, when Stephen Lane had told me that there were very few Morons props or costumes out there in the collecting world, he perhaps didn't realise that he, himself, might well have been sat in the same room as Mel's actual helmet as he typed, since Propstore proudly display a full Outland spacesuit in their office. Maybe he should check it for snot.

Maybe I'm thinking too much about Morons From Outer Space.

AN UNEXPECTED ENDING

I'm in Griff Rhys Jones's house. By invitation – don't worry. After I contacted his agent, his personal assistant, seemingly out of the blue, has emailed to tell me that Griff would be happy to do an interview. A week later, here I am, sat with a very amiable Griff in his study – a room full of books and shelves and comfy old furniture. Without a shred of ostentation, it is filled with the trophies of an interesting life. I see no mementoes from Morons. Griff is just finishing up his run on the West End stage in Moliere's The Miser and wears Harpagon's waxed moustache and imperial beard even in his downtime.

I have to say, I was worried about this meeting. I don't tend to get nervous before interviews, people are people, but this isn't just an interview. I'm worried that Griff will think that my aim is to mock, to hold Morons up for ridicule. I wonder why he even agreed to the interview. I wonder if I would. If somebody wanted to interview me about something I had done thirty years ago which was not considered a success. But Griff greets me with a big smile and a handshake and immediately tells me that he's very happy right now as my interview request inspired him to invite Mike Hodges to lunch the previous day and how wonderful it had been to catch up with him. We sit down to talk and Griff mentions that he has just got hold of a copy of Morons to watch in preparation for the interview but didn't get a chance to watch it. So, I ask, when was the last time he saw the film?

"1986? 1985...", he shrugs, "No, I've never seen it again since we finished it, I think. I don't think there's ever been a reason for seeing it. I've had no compunction to see it again, particularly because it's something where you go "Well, it's not working, nobody wants it, there's nothing we can do with it, let's just move on". You *have* to get to that state. You have to say "OK, they don't like it, let's move on.""

So, it looks like we're getting straight into it. He's brought it up, so I have to ask him, what happened? Why didn't it work? He stops and thinks for a moment.

"It was to do with being green, it was to do with being – at the time – successful, because of Not The Nine O'Clock News, it was to do with, I think, moving some of the tropes that we found funny into that world without really testing them through and going "What does an audience want?" but, mainly it was to do with *not enough work on the script.*"

He emphasizes those last six words.

"I feel that what happened was that we went with a script which we'd worked on and we went to people who were not experienced in low comedy, broad comedy. That was Verity (Lambert) and Bob Mercer who were running EMI. They'd quite recently taken over. And, so, people liked the big idea and they liked the script and they trusted us and, frankly, I think, we should have done two things. First of all, we should have been sent back to rewrite it many more times. Then, since you're on your way to making a big film, there would have been no harm to bring in other gag-writers. To go "Let's go through this with a fine tooth comb and make this more solid". So, I think the reason there was stickiness between Mike and us was because we had recently come out of a much more wham-bam television process of telling jokes, and a much faster-moving medium. So, there were lots of things along the way which became… our inexperience and everybody's inexperience at making this sort of film. Including Mike's. So, under those circumstances, what you really need to do is spend a bit of time looking at other films and going "What works here? What doesn't work? What should we do?" In other words, there was the general arrogance of two thirty-year-olds coming out of quite a successful television show. But, this is the other thing about Morons which is quite interesting; if you're making a broad parody, low comedy… *fuck the plot.*"

He lets the words hang there for a moment.

"The plot is of no purpose or interest. It's like a form of pornography. In Airplane, the plot is written already – the plane is in trouble, it's coming down, nobody has to worry about the plot. What's funny in Airplane is the people coming in, the circumstances are there, there's no real development, you don't have to listen to what happens, because each scene you've absolutely seen before. And now, what we're getting is a series of crazy jokes about that. Comedy pornography. From one big cum shot to the next cum shot. That's what you're doing. We don't want them walking up to the house or saying anything unless it's developing towards these moments of hilarity. You don't need any complexity. There's another form of comedy – the Ealing form of comedy – which can be very funny and is greatly respected, which is a situational comedy, about plot development, and this plot is the thing which makes it funny because we're dealing with characters who have real problems, however crudely expressed they are, but they are not going to be involved in low jokes or huge crazy things happening, they're actually going to be involved in a level of observation that you're looking for in the comedy. Strong comic-plot-driven story." Now. Morons, and this is our inexperience, Morons had a complex plot. Quite an interesting plot. You can imagine Morons being remade as a much more Galaxy Quest type story. Without the attempts at major, big jokes, but actually concentrating all the while on finessing the story to find the funniest things that would happen in plot development. You could even see it being made as a straight film – the thing that we make contact with is just an interstellar truck and doesn't have anything to tell us about the world. That premise could work. But what happened was that we were in a hybrid. So, when it was seen by American executives, they said "What happened to the jokes? It starts like Airplane or a Mel Brooks film and then suddenly it just stops." And we go "We're trying to tell the story!" And they go "WHY?"

Before we'd sat down, Griff had warned me that he can talk. And he really can, he talks in long, eloquent, often hilarious outbursts but then stops and thinks for a bit before continuing. These little moments of contemplation would be awkward but I realize that he's gathering his thoughts. He clearly has so much to say on the subject and he takes care in working out how to express it. This pause is an awkward one, though. He looks at me for a moment as if he's sizing me up, as if he's sure he wants to say what's on his mind or, more likely, it turns out, how to say it without being misunderstood. He bows his head and continues carefully:

"This is a weird thing. Because I want to take more credit for a complete failure than is often given to me. I was really the writer on it. Mel didn't really write much. And he never wrote anything for Smith & Jones, you know? So, the two of us had written some stuff together, but I was the principal. I had written, if you like, some good gags and I'd written quite an interesting plot and, even then, having got to that stage, having been a radio producer, and worked in comedy for some time, I was agitating for more work on the script. I don't think we'd have ever solved the problem. Trying to be all things to all people in one film is a really compli-cated thing. We got the whole thing going, we went away to Italy, another interesting sort of element to it. And Mel was always a restless guy to start with, because he just wanted it done. You know? And it was a mistake to go away, the two of us. It was the last thing we ever wrote together, really. It was just, you know, we went on working together for another 17 years but during all that time, it was never a good idea to put the two of us, actually for long periods of time in the same caravan, or whatever. We were very different people in some respects. We loved each other, but it just wasn't. I remember it not being hugely successful but we did all the work and we wrote the first draft, and they liked the first draft and they obviously liked the storyline. And then the railroad starts…"

"OK", I say, "Let me just ask, you'd never – either of you – written a full screenplay before? Did you do any preparation for that?"

"We had written a lot of sketches together for Not The Nine O' Clock News."

"Sure, but that's not a 90 minute screenplay."

"Nooooo. No. Exactly! That's it."

"And you didn't feel, while you were writing it like you needed some help, that you were struggling…?"

"No, we didn't feel like that. We were pretty young, and pretty comfortable, and it was a different business, you know? In those days. I think if we'd been working in Hollywood, we would have had a different experience, but we were working in Britain. And we started to put down on the page something that looked like a film. But it was also in comedy. And it was also in this period."

"And, at this time, there was a tradition of the transfer of British TV comedians to film – Kenny Everett made a film, Cannon and Ball, On The Buses…"

"Yes, people did this sort of thing. But it had quite epic reach. There were loads of big ideas in this film. There's a rocket landing on a motorway and a rocket up in space... It had potential. And I think everybody recognized that it had potential. And, I feel most guilty about not being able to... about not taking another six months to write more drafts and not looking at it. You know, it was just something thing that was happening alongside a lot of other things that were happening as well. And, actually, in retrospect, now, I realize that it was a big thing to decide that we could write a screenplay against those circumstances, without actually having paid much attention to the business of writing screenplays."

I ask him to take me all the way back to the beginning to unpick the actual origin of the project.

"Uh, it came out of the idea that there should be a film coming out of Not The Nine O'Clock News, However, Not The Nine O'Clock News had sort of come to an end, not acrimoniously, but it sort of got to a point where it fractured into different groups of people moving on. It wasn't going to happen with Rowan (Atkinson), because Rowan was already being urged by voices, I don't know what they were, one of them was his agent, to separate himself from Not The Nine O'Clock News, not to be associated with the other people and to pursue a solo career. Pamela (Stephenson) had also heard voices – I don't know if they were internal, or voices from space, saying "You must also have a solo career, Pamela", so Mel & I were both producers, Mel had been producing shows on the Fringe, directing them, and I'd been a producer for BBC radio, and we both sat there and said "We're coming to the end of this hugely successful show and we're now just bringing it to an end and we're doing that because Pam and Rowan want to go on and do more hugely successful shows." And they'd never been in anything but a hugely successful show: by that stage Mel and I had already been in failures! So we weren't quite so happy with the idea of saying "Oh, we're in a huge success, we've done four series, that's enough, let's finish!" Mel and I had already gravitated together, partly because it's like being in an insane asylum, and we sat there slightly world-weary. We went to [series producer] John Lloyd, but he was extremely picky what he got involved in, so was Rowan, they wanted nothing more to do with us anymore, so we just went ahead. We went ahead, I think. If John had been involved, it would have been a good idea. I don't think we ever formally invited him to join this thing, but what had happened was that there had been a discussion, but they would never have joined in an idea that we had presented. If we presented Morons from Outer Space and said "We're going to make this film", they would never have got involved. All I can remember is that there was talk of a film and I had had this storyline idea about the aliens arriving. And also, this sense that it would be fun to do because there was a lot of space movies around at that time. And nobody had made a parody. It just seemed that there was a target. Universal put money into it... so, my honeymoon was spent in Los Angeles, just about the only time I've ever been to Los Angeles, and Mel came too and we went to see somebody really big – Barry Diller, somebody like that, and we were surprised by how cool he was about meeting us, and he wanted to know if we knew Richard Curtis! So, that's all I really remember about it, was that he was eager to talk about Richard Curtis to us."

Griff laughs at this. Takes a drink and composes himself.

"The thing that I always felt about Morons From Outer Space, this is the real thing, having been effectively the person who wrote the plot, wrote the story, wrote the idea, the satirical element about a group of morons who crashed their spaceship, through inadequacy on earth, and then been made into this incredible pop group, while one of them – this was also a parody of spaceship stories –

because there are plenty of alien stories where the aliens are just like human beings and if you've got nothing to prove you are an alien, you're a nut, but if you happened to be at the controls of a spaceship, you're somebody extraordinary."

He's not looking at me. He's looking into the middle distance. When he looks back to me, it is with intensity.

"With more intelligent, clever and interesting people, we'd have thought of better jokes and put it into some sort of shape, but I always thought it was a great idea. So for a long time, I wanted to actually make the straight version of this. If I had my life all over again, I would do this film again!"

I was not expecting that. He registers this, nods and continues.

"I would make the film with this story. It needs to be remade by a more competent team, not necessarily director, but a more competent team of writers to say "This is the story that is in this rather interesting sort of melange." Because, yes, we did throw the kitchen sink. We just reached around for anything and flung it on, we were so inexperienced."

Again, he pauses and nods to himself.

"So, I'm afraid, yes, there is that element of throwing the kitchen sink in., I think if it had been more radically out there, with even more crazy things happening, space calamities and jokes and things like that, and we'd sat down and spent a good three weeks doing nothing but watching sci-fi movies and then putting every single trope, every single cliché, in, we'd have been better than trying to finesse the story, which actually is a distraction. But, the story is an interesting story!"

I ask him about the title, Mike Hodges had mentioned to me that he hated the title and felt it had been detrimental to the film's success. That he had preferred the original title 'Illegal Aliens'.

"No, no, I think it was maybe called Illegal Aliens first as a working title, then Morons. I can't remember."

He suddenly starts laughing. Really laughing. I have no idea what he's laughing about.

"I still find the title funny!" he guffaws.

He continues laughing. It's infectious. I'm laughing now too. It is, actually, a really funny title.

I ask him who the film was made for, what audience did they have in mind? That it seemed aimed at children in some places and yet it featured some very dark stuff and a sex scene.

"There wasn't any discussion about that. As there might be today, and there probably was in America. This was a film that was being made, as it were, for... us. Once it was being made by EMI, they wanted a certificate that would take it out to as broad an audience as possible, that meant, because of the popular success of Not The Nine O'Clock News, that probably meant that they wanted it to allow kids to go and see it. It was a pretty juvenile film, wasn't it? I think Mel and I always wanted a general audience. We laughed at broad humour and we liked jokes and stuff. We were castigated for not being alternative enough and I wouldn't say we were mainstream, but yet we never had that urge to be hip. It wasn't a question of making a niche film. And you couldn't at this budget. The idea was to make entertainment. The idea was to get into the Mel Brooks world, that sort of thing."

I start to push him for more specifics but he cuts me off.

"There wasn't any thinking, I'm afraid. I wish I could say... you might notice as time goes on that there wasn't... enough... thinking... done around this film. A bit more thinking would have probably been a much better thing. Instead of just rushing to do what we had to do. It certainly burned our fingers and made us that bit more weary of doing things at the time. You will ask me details of the film, but... I can't even remember that there *was* a sex scene. I think... that's the scene where Joanne was being screwed by Jimmy and was eating an apple while he's doing it? Yes, well, that would be the sort of thing that would set us off, and I remember it distinctly, being on set and going "No, don't do that! Don't do that, it's not necessary."

"So, was that coming from Mike? Where was that coming from?"

"I don't know. Probably from Mike. Once the film started shooting, we did feel separate from the process as writers and, in order to talk to Mike, I think maybe Mike had had enough by then of being with writers, every director does, he was going to make his own film. And there were moments where, if you look back at the tension that started on the film, there was no more than any other comedy, comedy is a difficult thing to work out. But we would have said... Anyway, you got a 'tea cosy effect' here, people are putting things on top of perfectly reputable jokes, they're adding things, everybody from the props man to the costume team are thinking "I can make this funny by adding this" and that, that's what's frustrating you. And it was frustrating us. Then this producer, Johnny Dark, was brought in during the making of Morons to bring it in on budget, I don't think he'll be credited. He's called an end producer, or a completion producer, he's brought in by the company and the insurance people because the thing is going over budget. So, you bring in this producer, and when he comes in, his job is, as an experienced producer, to say to the guys making this film "You're going over budget and we're going to need you to finish this film by doing this..." And it's brutal, because he comes in, takes pages out of the script, throws away this idea, and this stuff that's not filmed, you'll just have to work around this."

"So, you had no control on this?"

"No, once the shoot had started, unless we were absolutely in the scenes, we felt very much like, I remember that, we felt that we couldn't... Now, this is really important – I have absolutely every sympathy with Mike and in my experience of making films now, I've learned it's better to get your fights done over the script before you start to shoot. Number one. Number two, let the director make the film that they want to make, or let the writers make the film that they want to make but don't get into a position where they're not quite in agreement over it. Mike was quite influenced by Jacques Tati, and we would come on and not recognize this. The whole basketball thing which he had done, which was brilliant, was not in the script and so there are things coming into the script that we, as writers, hadn't seen! And at one point, I remember distinctly, that we tried to film a misprint, and I can't remember what it was, and we said "No, no, that's not." and people said "But we find this really funny!" and we said "No, no, it's a misprint, it's not... it's not 'fine', it's 'fire'!" or something like that. So, it's complicated to talk about. It was a massive film. When it's made, it's massively complex, it had huge sets and Mel and I would walk on and go "What the fuck is this???" and they'd say "This is the set for..." and you go "OH... My God. We hadn't conceived it as being like this." So, what's interesting, and it's really, really important that this is not a criticism of Mike, because it's not just that we got together the other day, it was very true that I hugely admire Mike, I really like him and he's the most decent person ever and he is not to blame for the faults with Morons

From Outer Space – I'm to blame for the faults from Morons From Outer Space."

He fixes me with a serious stare.

I ask him to elaborate on the tensions between Hodges and him and Mel.

"What I remember was some of the confusions, the things that happened. I need to watch it again and see what I recognize and don't recognize and where these touch points were, but we had also come from television cutting. I wouldn't have done this these days, but stupidly we'd say to Mike "Oh, you need to zoom in here" or something like that, stupid, bad things, crude, not knowing how films work. Around the edit, things like that. Needing close-ups on things and seeing things happening, and his experience with a big screen would have probably been stronger than ours. But there are sequences, aren't there, that work very well? I'm talking to somebody, I hope, who is a fan of things that were done well. Jimmy Nail is very funny in it, isn't he?"

I agree, Jimmy Nail is fantastic in it. I ask him what his reaction was to the critical response to the film.

"Oh, devastated. Mel was always a much more steady person than I was. He was very steady, very cool guy. And so, it didn't register in much the same way, but it was very bad. The truth is, it was devastating. The trouble is that Morons desperately affected my life. I mean, I love film and I see loads of films and I would have loved to have worked with film and get myself better at it and to learn how to make films and all of that stuff. As it happened, Mel had fierce ambition, and sort of left me holding the baby, is the truth. He left me holding Smith & Jones. Thirteen series. I was left flogging on and Mel decided "Well, I'm going to be a film director", so he went off and he did it! When your partner goes off and becomes a film director, you can't go "I'm going to be a film director too!" People do dwell on these things. Because they're wounding, they're hurtful, they really are. They diminish. By the nature of bad reviews, they demean what you do. As a human being. So, it was a pity. It didn't strike any chords in America at all. "The film sucks" came back from the preview cards. They recorded, with delight, that the preview cards in America had been very, very low. They said "Look at this! We can't remember a film recently that has done as badly as this!" And asked for comments, people in the audience said things like "This film sucks" but that was partly a reaction – I'll take a reaction from Mel's film Blackball, it's an interesting film, it came out around the same time as Dodgeball and it's a very similar story. In Blackball, he's playing bowls, and in Dodgeball, they turn Dodgeball into a big sport and do a silly version of that. It's the losers making the top rung. In Mel's film, the loser was like a real loser, Paul Kaye, the guy who played Dennis Pennis, he is a very skilful actor and he plays a cunt, he plays a loser, a man who is unpleasant. Then the whole point of the film, cynically, which is a bit of a laugh, is that this man who nobody likes becomes champion. But its not a feel-good experience. In Dodgeball, with Ben Stiller, its got a group of disabled people – they have some things that Mel and I would have gone "We're not putting up with this shit!" "We love you, remember you're real human beings!" It's all lovely, and their victory is a feel-good victory. I won't give people that sentimental, pathetic Richard Curtis side, this is not meant as a criticism of Richard either, Richard is good at that, Richard puts in the disabled people, Richard actually has love in his films, he wants it to be an emotional film. Mel's film was a hard-edged film, it lacks that belief, because Mel lacked that, didn't want that, didn't believe in that, didn't like that. Would have watched a film and gone "Bleurgh" when he saw that happen. But that's what people like. Morons is a cynical film. Cynicism is written all over it. There's nobody to like in it. There's no heartwarming moment.

Everything is seen as being slightly depraved. It's an English reserve, it's an English thing, actually, people do love each other, it's funny isn't it? It's sort of like silly and needs to be undercut and cynically we don't want this to happen. And that is so interesting because Blackball is a perfectly well made film, but it lacks the heart that Dodgeball had and as a result had difficulty finding an audience. So, no, Morons was a real kick in the goolies, you know? A real "Fucking hell, we've really fucked up here and I don't want to revisit this, I don't want to go through this hell again." Success – when everybody's working together, you've got the right idea and you know what the parameters are – is actually quite enjoyable and quite easy. If you really want hard work, try shining a piece of shit. Try working on something which isn't quite working and you can't work out why. That's hard work. That is hard work. And, actually, Morons was quite hard work. We thought "We've got something here", but there was a dissatisfaction as we were making it, with "What are we doing wrong?" It's instructive to be in mega-flops."

"So, why have you not pursued cinema? You could still be in films!"

"No, I can't. You know it's not as easy as that. And I, did for a long while, work on various scripts and big ideas, and they've all become nearly-projects. I've never been without work. I've worked and done a lot of work in the theatre, I've produced a film about the death of Dylan Thomas, Tom Hollander won the Best Actor RTS award, we won BAFTAs – Welsh BAFTAs, it was a big success and hilariously we've not been able to get anything off the ground since. So, it's as difficult to follow a huge success as it is to follow a shitpile. It was a small film, right out of the traps, we did everything right, got everything right, that put people's noses out of joint. It's a funny, funny old world."

So, I ask him, what has he done since?

"I've sort of ended up being in production for a bit, I just ended up making a lot of factual stuff recently, some of which has been good and fun to do. I realized around the year 2000 that the BBC weren't interested in me as a comedian anymore, so I said, "It's alright, don't worry", I got on a boat and I sailed away. I got as far as Denmark when I got a call from my agent saying "They want you to do a show called Restoration" so I came back and did that, but if I hadn't, I'd be sailing around the world. I seriously had decided to just fuck off. And then I set up a company and did that show for 10 years and we made lots of things, we piled them all up, I've been round the world making films about mountains, rivers, trains, God knows what. And then, suddenly last year, people asked me to be in plays. And the trouble with making documentaries for the BBC is that you're constantly waiting, they'll say, "Oh yeah, we love this, we're going to do this, go away and do more work on it." And you do more work and say, "Have you made a decision on it yet? And they say, "No, someone's changing jobs at the moment, so it's alright, we really love it" but nothing happens. So I got all these offers to do things but had to say "No, I've got this company". Finally last year I said "Fuck this, I can't just go on dutifully keeping people employed. Stop." So, off I went back to the theatre. Maybe I've got a few years left to play around in theatre. And in the meantime, I haven't got a company, I must sit down and write my screenplays. Ideas for things come along but I'm not a great screenplay writer. Not an experienced enough screenplay writer. And really, I think now looking back, you need to have the courage to say "I can put this together, but I need to put a good team together" and do it that way."

There is a finality to what he says, but I do still have some questions to ask about Morons and I'm not going to waste the opportunity.

"Why don't the two principals meet until the very end?" I ask. "What's the thought behind that?"

"No thought. No thought. Not enough thought. NOT. ENOUGH. THINKING."

"But, It's a Mel Smith and Griff Rhys Jones film!"

"YES!"

"And yet, you're not the stars…?"

"NO! No! But also the thinking was it would be selfless of us and it'd be recognized to be selfless for us not to try to be like two buddies off the tv doing things together."

"So is that one of the crucial mistakes of the film? That you don't share screen time together?

"Well, it may be. It's a Mel Smith & Griff Rhys Jones film and you go to see a double act doing their thing and then they're not working together. And that *was* a mistake, probably. These mistakes, you look back in hindsight and go "Yeah, well, that's a very silly mistake". *Never occurred to us.* Never occurred."

"I genuinely, into my teenage assumed that the whole point of Morons was that it was the story of how you and Mel met, and that when you meet each other at the end, in the stadium, that that was the joke."

"That they'd go off and the two of us would be together from then on? Yes, of course, that is the joke!"

"Oh, that IS the joke???"

"Well, of course! At one level, that's a sort of internal joke. It's not worth putting a whole movie at fault for that one joke! That just shows our arrogance! Mel and I did a sketch in the last series. About working in our office and somebody comes in – a junior – comes in and says "Deirdre's leaving the office, she's going on maternity leave and would you just write in her card?". We go "OK, *which one is she*?" So we open the card, look at the card and start reading what other people have written, these warm, funny tributes to Deirdre. Witty things. Mel sits there chewing the end of a pen and I say "Come on let's just write something down!" This is a sketch I'd written, only because this is what happens when you work in an office. So, later in the programme we cut back and it's past midnight, we're still sitting in the office, and we're reading out the ones we've come up with and none of them are appropriate or funny, so then we cut again and this time we've got twelve writers in the room and we're sitting with twelve writers and they're all giving us their ideas for different things for the card. People put absurdly obscene stuff in and would say "No, that worked, honestly – you can see how the sketch worked – and then somebody comes up with a great idea and Mel says "That's the one we'll do" and they look at the card and it's already there, somebody's already written it. And the final scene is when Deirdre comes back into the room and somebody says "Deirdre, how lovely to see you!" and she's already had the baby and is back from maternity leave. And this was reviewed and the reviewer said "With no apparent irony, Mel Smith and Griff Rhys Jones get 12 writers in to write one card." And you go, "No. I hope you don't mind, that's with APPARENT irony. That's with... IRONY! THAT WHOLE THING IS ABOUT WRITING SKETCH SHOWS! THAT'S WHAT IT'S ABOUT, YOU CUNT! HOW CAN YOU WRITE THAT? THAT IS A STATEMENT! THAT IS A STATEMENT ABOUT CYNICISM! ABOUT OURSELVES AND WHAT WE ARE! Everything we did in Smith & Jones was at that level. We only went back and did more of it because every time it went out, it'd get huge ratings! So they'd say "Make more!" "Alright, we'll make more, because we've got a company, got hundreds of people sitting around, it has to happen every year."

He sighs.

"Oh dear. And that's the thing, in a way we were a terrible pair of cynical people about the business, about what we'd been though. The worst crashing defeats to our egos, we'd experienced it all! And also, the crushing business of staring at a blank piece of paper because you've got to get something done. Hack work, the fact that it's all fun for the first four years but then everyone takes up drugs or whatever because they're so bored of just getting on with it, and seemingly its all work, work, work all that thing. It's funny, very funny now, because I'm in the theatre and it's like joining a children's party in terms of enthusiasm and loveliness. People baking cakes every day and I turn up and say hello to everybody and vow undying friendship and do the warm ups and you know jolly together. I think "Well, it's great, it's lovely, it's really good" but Mel and I never had any of that! Any we're-all-in-the-jolly-world-of-show-business shit. And so, that unfortunate hard edge, that edge of cynicism, that edge of "You'll laugh at this because its a bad title – it's *deliberately* a bad title! It's not like we could have had good titles, could have had a much more acceptable title, no, we've *chosen deliberately* a title which will slightly annoy you by talking about morons and actually taking an attitude both to cinema and their titles. And that we have a sneaking regard for things called Return of the Toxic Avenger, we quite liked schlock and also something slightly offensive as well. We've never failed to offend people. Not offend people by being offensive, doing gross-out jokes – but just by doing things that you know are not sentimental and don't have any pathos in them or character depth or things like that. It's not that we can't do it – it's just that we don't want to! It's not quite the same thing. And then to be accused of not being able to do it, you just go "No, you just don't understand! Its nothing to do with that!" We should have given them some scenes of pathos."

"Mel had pathos!" I protest.

"Mel had pathos. Mel did, and that's why he comes across as the most sympathetic story, in a funny sort of way. You look at Judd Apatow's films and they're constantly "I've got really big problems", now we're going to do something absurd, but now's the scene where I talk about the trouble I had at my wedding." And you look at Dodgeball and it's even cruder – a very crude mix of sympathy for disabled people and then silly comedy in the middle of it."

Griff thinks about it for a second and then leans in:

"If you want success, you have to actually bake a cake according to the recipe sometimes. This was going into the finale of The Great British Bake Off without a recipe, thinking you could rewrite the recipe for a Victoria Sponge. You can't rewrite the recipe. There are some rules you need to stick to."

Which pretty much sums it all up, doesn't it? The whole Morons From Outer Space venture.

But I still have some questions left. All of the stupid little things which I've wondered for years or that have come up during the process of writing this book. I ask him if we can just do them quickfire to get them out of the way. He nods. I begin.

Who is Simon Bell?
"Oh Simon! Now, Simon is an old mate, I was at school with Simon, he was two years below me and he was a very good friend of Mel's, and so he was a guy who was hanging around, he was a writer, so he wrote the novelization."

"Was he married to someone called Margaux?"

"No, I don't think so. I don't think he's ever been married."

I explain the signed dedication that had been detailed in the second-hand copy on Amazon.

"Really? What the fucking hell? It's written in it? I had no idea that he was married, Simon. I can't imagine he ever was, he's such a bachelor figure. Wait, I know what that is – that's somebody's bought the book to give to Margaux, it's not a dedication by Simon…"

"It's signed Simon Bell."

"Well, when I see him, I shall ask him. I wish I could tell you, but I can't."

Do you know who Fred Wood is?
"No."

I explain about the supporting-artist wormhole that I had fallen down following the BBFC report about Fred's 'willly'

"Right. I wouldn't have been involved in any way in the casting or the decisions about what he did. I don't even remember the scene, but as I say, I haven't seen it in thirty years. When you leave, I'm going to pluck up enough courage to sit down and watch this film."

Why is only Mel's face on the poster?
"Uh, I don't know. I don't know."

"Just because it's a double act, it seems like it would be the two of you."

"Yes, but it was Smith & Jones, Mel & Griff. I was always the oily rag of the relationship. In Laurel & Hardy, Stan Laurel did all the work and Oliver Hardy played golf. And in Smith & Jones, Mr Jones did most of the arguing with the producers and fitting it all out, and Mel would turn up and do the show and that's how he was happy to do it. We were lucky if he turned up some days, but that was fantastic. I'm not belittling him, that's the way it works out in partnerships and that's absolutely fine. But we would go into meetings and people would almost automatically talk to Mel first and address him. He just had the presence of being the senior figure, the older brother. You know what I mean? That's maybe what that was, but I don't know – this is the sort of point, swallowing the toad, to use Norman Lewis's phrase, putting up with this unpleasant sort of thing where you just have to say "OK, that's the way it is" and that was one of those things where I probably went "…OK" I don't remember it being an issue at any time with me. I think it was just pleasing to see it."

Can we talk about the science of Morons From Outer Space?
"There wasn't any science in it!"

I tell him about my conversation with Brian Mackenwells and that he thought that the Morons themselves were quite in keeping with what scientists currently believe aliens might be like.

Griff chuckles at this. "OK"

"Brian wants to know this; why do the scientists take their helmets off?

"Probably because Mike wanted to see their faces. It's the sort of thing that we wouldn't be able to answer."

Did you keep any mementoes from Morons From Outer Space?

"No, no, I don't think so. I'm not a big mementoes man. I'm just wondering if there is anything I could help you with, but I will have a look around – there might be a script somewhere. I wouldn't know where. Or where I put it. Or why I kept it. Oooh. I'll tell you what there is! In the very early days of thinking it through, I drew a sort of storyboard of how it opened."

"And you still have that?"

"Somewhere. Isn't that funny, I was looking at it a little while ago. I wonder whether it is… it was just a sort of notebook. I'd obviously started work thinking about it, this is way, way before we even wrote the script, some of the ideas about how it would be presented. I ought to have a search to see…"

Griff gets up and starts searching through cupboards.

"The only thing that's interesting, if it were here… I have a lot of books to look through. Oh, wait a minute, look! Here it is! Yes. I haven't seen this, but…"

He pulls out a dusty old sketchbook and thumbs through to the Morons section. Five pages of rather beautifully drawn storyboards which are pretty true to the opening of the actual film. His rendering of the massive spaceship with the little caravan towed at the back by a chain is detailed and impressive. The second joke of the film – Des getting his oxygen tube shut in the door is there and the spacewalk he does to get back to the main ship. This is obviously long before casting as Des is a large man with a big moustache rather than Jimmy Nail.

"That's really accurate to how it came out!" I squeal.

"Yeah? That was my idea for the first joke."

"Which is still there!"

"Is it?"

"Yeah, of course! That's Jimmy Nail, that's the opening."

"And, at that time, it was called The Space Invaders. So, those were all the original jokes. Isn't that funny? It was just like that. Have that. That was lucky. That was a very, very early stage of me working through my story. I should have done the whole thing like that, shouldn't I? And then the film would have stayed at the same level."

"The drawing is very accurate to the model – they must have given this to the model makers."

"No, nobody saw that. No."

Why does Matteson suddenly burst into song when the aliens escape?

"We… must have thought it was funny. You're spoiling it for me now! This needs a spoiler alert. What does he do? What does he sing?"

"A song about Sandra."

"Oh, because he's in love with Sandra? Wow. We were cheeky, weren't we? To put that sort of thing in. And is that Dinsdale playing Matteson? Again, you see, what I remember is we started to make the plot more complex than it needed to be… how bizarre. That's a late-night writing session, somebody coming up with a crazy idea."

Was there ever talk of a sequel?

"Five years after we made the film, we get a phone call from a guy who's coming over from America, wants to come to see us, what does he want? Our agent says, "He wants to see you because he is an American property developer in New York and his best friend owns video shops and every week, they sit down and watch Morons From Outer Space," because this guy was apparently talking to his friend and said, "What film should I watch?" and his friend said "You must watch this film, it's one of the least valued, and it is a crazy film" and he had come over to make a film with us!"

Griff laughs to himself.

"With a million quid that he wanted to put on the table to get this film started. And he came over, stayed in The Dorchester, I remember we went to see him there, going "You're nuts. That's crazy!" Now I look back on it and say, "We should have!" but Mel, at the time, didn't want to get involved with it particularly. Mel was now totally wary of going through the same experience as that and was already thinking about how he could become a film director and not do things with me. So, in a funny way, that was one of those things – in the Dorchester, a man literally ready to write a cheque for a million pounds and get to work, and we were being naïve, now I think about it. Actually, a million pounds start up, bring in other money, probably could have made another film, so you go 'Wow', but what was really fascinating was to find out there was this guy who ran a video store who recommended people Morons From Outer Space! "Oh right, so you're a fan of this film?" He said "Yeah, we watch it all the time, we always get drunk and sit around and laugh at it". Great. We didn't go and look at it again and say "I wonder what that's like", we just went "OK"

He remembers something else.

"Bob Mercer was quite drunk one night and he said "you know, we'd be perfectly happy to make Morons 2" and I said "What?" he said "Yeah, yeah, it made enough money." I notice in one of the things you've said that it was a box-office failure, but I don't think it was. If you go on Wikipedia, it says its British income was only 3.5 or something like that, but worldwide it obviously made a profit. And was popular in parts of the world that we don't know anything about. I don't think it was the film that sunk EMI. It was quite an expensive film to make and it wasn't a hit, and I was staggered by Bob saying that. I said "Morons 2?" He said "Yeah, yeah, we should get going on it, you should start writing it, because the first one wasn't big but there's enough money in people liking it to go and make a sequel, if you want to do it". I think, again, we said "No, no! We can't go through that again!" That's how traumatized I was by what happened. It killed me to the bottom of my soul.

How often do you think about Morons From Outer Space?
"Very rarely."

That's the end of my list of questions. The end of my journey. From sitting in an empty cinema at nine years old, being entranced by this bizarre film, to sitting in the home of its de facto creator holding the sketchbook containing the first moment of its creative work three decades later. But I realize that I have one more thing that I really want to ask him.

"Why did you agree to this interview?"

"I've spent a lot of time recently doing a show about Mel, which I took around the country and so as a result of doing that, I've been thinking back about a few things, you know? That we did together. And one of them was this very strange experience of making Morons From Outer Space. What an experience. To really be the very first experience of making a film is to make a thing as ambitious and over-ambitious and as silly and over-the-top as that. With huge crashes on the motorway and however many weeks it was we spent shooting. That's the reason. So, there is an element of me that feels it will be nice in the long term, and particularly nice for Mike, really, that it didn't get treated as a complete waste of time. And that just makes me feel a little warmer about... my... wasted life."

He laughs with a silly "ki-ki-ki-ki-ki" and flashes me a massive grin. I thank him.

"Well, thank you for showing an interest in it! The only thing I don't want out of this is to be put in a position of having to defend it again. You know what I mean? It's that thing where you go and meet people – or you did at the time – and they would say to you "Why did you make this terrible film?" and you'd go "Well, I don't know why we made it!" and I feel really sorry for the mistakes we made and how juvenile we were about things as we were doing it and, if I had the time again... you know? But, no doubt one would just make different mistakes."

"Well, for my part", I tell him "Morons has always brought joy into my life."

"I'm glad that you're proselytizing on behalf of us. Now, after all these years. And Mel would be so chuffed."

He laughs loudly and slaps the arm of the sofa.

I emerge from Griff's house into the blinding light of an early summer day in central London and realise I have a massive grin on my face. But then, Morons From Outer Space will do that to me.

ACKNOWLEDGEMENTS

My biggest thanks have to go to Griff Rhys Jones without whom, of course, this book would not exist. For the years of enjoyment that Morons have brought me, even though it didn't do the same for him, I am eternally grateful. More than that, the generosity of spirit displayed in welcoming into his home a shabby stranger and spending hours, candidly and with great humour, discussing what could be considered his biggest artistic failure. I hope this book might warm his heart towards Morons a little more.

Massive thanks to FRANK TURNER for his beautiful foreword. Our tastes in music have always been similar but to find out that the only other Morons evangeliser was so close to home was a heartwarming, and somewhat intellectually validating, moment. If you're not familiar with Frank's music, get familiar with it. He also wrote a great book called The Road Beneath My Feet, which should be checked out.

To SAM JORDISON, I send my gratitude once more. One couldn't hope for a greater editor, even if he uses his position to hide messages in my work berating me for my love of The Levellers (who, by the way, Frank also loves). Sam is a fantastic writer and I urge you all to seek out his new book Enemies Of The People. And all of his old books. If you like my stuff, you'll like his.

My proofreader is my mum, LAURA SPIRA. Her pride upon reading my first book was tempered by her fury for my grammatical abandon and decision to save a couple of quid by not having it proofread. She worked on this one for free. Although, I'm writing this section after she's finished. So, I's hoped there nomore mistkae and that your Still pride of me. Thank's mum.

HANK STARRS continues to be the creative opinion I seek out first and pay great heed to. Thanks go to him not only for his counsel but also for his massive enthusiasm which has buoyed me through the moments in which I realised I was actually, genuinely, writing a book about Morons From Outer Space.

This book would also not have been possible without the time and professional insight of:

STUART BARR
ANTON BITEL
LAURIE GOODE
MIKE HODGES
STEPHEN LANE
BRIAN MACKENWELLS

Or the support, influence and generosity of:

SARAH CURRANT
CLAIRE GEDDIE
KERRY MEECH
SARAH ROSCOE
JACOB SMITH

Or the artistry of:

PAUL LOUDON
ALISON SIDGWICK

To JEN (my soon-to-be wife) who is not one of the Morons From Outer Space, Jon Spira.

Seriously though, this book really couldn't have happened without Jen's emotional and practical support. She has celebrated in the high moments, comforted in the low moments and tolerated a living room full of what must surely be the biggest amassing in history of Morons From Outer Space crap. She puts up with a lot from this particular moron.

Last, but in absolutely no way least, the people who made this book a reality. My lovely Kickstarter backers and founder members of The Forgotten Film Club:

SIMON TRIGWELL / NICK DEAKIN / SIMON TAYLOR / PAUL SANDERS / HANK STARRS / SCOTT BISHOP / BOAZ HALACHMI / PHILL WARREN / JUSTIN RASMUSSEN T.J.DeCARLO / PETER "PIRATE" DAVID / MATTHEW STANOSZ / JACOB W. FLEMING / LIAM DUNNE / GARY LAWRENCE / GREG WINTER / SYLVIA FIEBIG / ANTONY BRIERS / ADAM NEWELL / KARMA CHRISTINE SALVATO / RICHARD PLUTHERO ANDERSON / COLIN VENTERS / FRU JEUNE / MARK SHADDOCK / TALLY & METZ / EON DAVIDSON / JONI SAVAGE / DAVID ELVIS LEEMING / JENS MANKEL / PAUL MOODY / TIM SHIELDS / STEVEN SEMPLE / MICHAEL MASSEY / MATT SEARLE / STEVEN WELLER / D VICKERS / NEIL KENNY / GAVIN WILSON / DEREK J. BALLING / ALAN STEPHEN / CHRIS L. WHITE / REVEK / SIMON WHITE / CHRIS JANES / STUART NAISMITH / TYLER GOODISON / ANDY MALT / BRYAN R. MARSHALL / JOHN MAZZEO / GAZ TIDEY / ANDREW ROPER / SARAH PALING / RICHARD BOWN / @P3RF3KT / CHRIS GEORGE / NORMAN PRIMROSE / ARRON CAPONE-LANGAN / TALIA KIMELMAN / AARON CATTERMER / JANIS BEST / TIM ELWELL / STEVE WELLS / NICK HARTLEY-SMITH / IAIN POTTER / ROSA LUXEMBURG / SIMON BLEAS-DALE / STUART ARNOTT / DAVID ESTALL / ERICA PRATT / GARDNER LINN / DEADLY / CHRIS EDWARDS / CLINT WILLIAMS / ANTHONY LAWRIE / ANDY HAIGH / GREG BARNES / SIMON HOGG / JAE COPE / DAN BOND / ROB THAY / SHERYLEE ANNE HOUSSEIN / ANDREW DAVID BARKER / ROBBIE WILSON / TARA HOWLEY / ROBERT WELLS / CHRISTIAN MONGGAARD / GEOFFD / ZAC PELKOWSKI / SCOTT SHAW / DARREN WHITING / ADAM CARL PARKER-EDMONDSTON / RON KOCHER / SASHA-JADE HORNBY / PAIGE RASMUSSEN / BRENT ZIUS / ROSS LAWHEAD / MALCOLM CLEUGH / SVEN GENGEL / IAN NURSER / ANDREW DYER / LARA WILSON /DARREN SAVAGE / DANIEL TREMBIRTH / SIMON J. PAINTER / MIKE SHEMA / SHANE DOYLE / CHRISTOPHER MITCHELL / STUART CAMPBELL / DANIEL C. HODGES / JUSTIN HARRIS / ADAM FULTON / BEN WADDELL / KAREN MELGAR / PAUL MARRIOTT

Follow Jon Spira at www.kickstarter.com to find out first about future projects.

If you enjoyed this book, please tell people about it and
give it a positive review. Thanks!

ABOUT THE AUTHOR

Jon Spira lives in North London with his partner, cat and several thousand DVDs.

He is a documentary filmmaker with two feature films to his name, ANYONE CAN PLAY GUITAR and ELSTREE 1976. He is currently making a sequel, ELSTREE 1979, which will be released in 2018.

Between 2013 and 2016, Jon was the in-house documentary filmmaker for the British Film Institute.

Over the years, Jon has been a film student, film tutor, film blogger, screenwriter and spent many years hanging out in, working, running or owning a wide variety of video shops.

His first book VIDEOSYNCRATIC: A BOOK ABOUT LIFE. IN VIDEO SHOPS was released in 2017 and is an odd-shaped book which looks exactly like a VHS tape.

He has written for The Huffington Post, BFI, Daily Telegraph and many crappy websites and blogs.

You can follow Jon on Twitter @videojon

To receive occasional information about Jon's future books and films, please sign up to his mailing list at:
http://eepurl.com/cD6-jX

You can check out his other work at:
www.jonspira.com